Glossary of Civil Resistance

**A RESOURCE FOR
STUDY AND TRANSLATION
OF KEY TERMS**

Front and back cover image:

Description: LGBT-Demonstration against the war in Ukraine and Russia in Saint-Petersburg. By: InkBoB. This image is licensed under a Creative Commons Attribution-ShareAlike 4.0 International (CC BY-SA 4.0). The image has been modified by cropping.

Link to license: https://creativecommons.org/licenses/by-sa/4.0/deed.en

Link to image: https://commons.m.wikimedia.org/wiki/File:LGBT-Demonstration_against_the_war_in_Ukraine_and_Russia_in_Saint-Petersburg.JPG

Front cover image:

Description: 2019 Hong Kong anti-extradition law protest on 21 July 2019. By: Studio Incendo. This image is licensed under a Creative Commons Attribution 2.0 Generic (CC BY 2.0). The image has been modified by cropping.

Link to license: https://creativecommons.org/licenses/by/2.0/deed.en

Link to image: https://commons.wikimedia.org/wiki/File:190721_HK_Protest_Incendo_04.jpg

This book was updated on April 14, 2021.

© 2021 International Center on Nonviolent Conflict
Hardy Merriman and Nicola Barrach-Yousefi
All rights reserved.
ISBN: 978-1-943271-31-3

Glossary of Civil Resistance

**A RESOURCE FOR
STUDY AND TRANSLATION
OF KEY TERMS**

Hardy Merriman
Nicola Barrach-Yousefi

With the assistance of
Julia Constantine and Kaileen McGourty

Contents

1   **Introduction**

11   **Key Terms List**

15   **Glossary**
Definitions, commentary, usage, and related terms

156   **Translations of Key Terms**

157   **Endnotes**

172   **Index**

174   **About the Authors**

Introduction

Civil resistance is everywhere. Virtually every country and society in the world has instances in their past—and sometimes their present—where people protested, boycotted, petitioned, went on strike, or engaged in other nonviolent actions to advocate for their rights. No one culture created civil resistance or owns it. It belongs to all of humanity.

Yet, this history is frequently unrecognized and not taught in schools. Resources to learn how to successfully organize, strategize, and engage in nonviolent struggle are often not widely available. In fact, some governments deliberately suppress or ban this knowledge.

The study of civil resistance focuses on how people can fight for—and win—their rights, freedom, and justice, without violence. There is great value in developing and sharing best practices, research, and educational resources about how to do this. The more people know, the more effective they can be as they adopt nonviolent strategies to challenge oppression.

The amount of English-language literature in this field has rapidly expanded in recent decades, and demand for materials in languages other than English has also risen. We created this glossary to help make this knowledge more available to people around the world. Its primary goal is to help with the translation of information on civil resistance from English into other languages.[i] We also believe that non-translators will find value in it, as a great deal can be learned by reading the definitions and commentary on each term.

---

[i] We would also love to see knowledge and case accounts that were originally published in other languages translated into English, and we encourage others to develop their own glossaries for their particular languages.

Why Translating in this Field is a Challenge

Translators do pioneering work, and there is power and responsibility in that role. It is always challenging to translate from one language to another, but materials on civil resistance can be particularly difficult, as well as interesting and exciting. Here are some reasons why:

1. **In some languages, terminology to describe nonviolent struggle is unclear or does not exist.**

    Originally, English had virtually no precise terminology to explain civil resistance. In the early 20th century, as Mohandas Gandhi sought to describe a technique of popular nonviolent struggle to English-speaking audiences, he found he had to create new terminology such as "civil resistance" (which is used to this day, with a meaning that has evolved over time). Gandhi also used terms that already existed but were uncommon, such as "civil disobedience" and "passive resistance" (a term he later abandoned). For Indian audiences, he coined the new word *satyagraha* ("truth-force") by combining the Sanskrit words for "truth" (*satya*) and "holding firmly to" (*agraha*).[ii] Over decades, English-speaking practitioners and scholars have continued to create new terminology—including terms such as "nonviolent conflict," "nonviolent action," "political defiance," and "people power"—to describe civil resistance.

    We frequently hear that equivalent terminology does not exist in

---

ii   Gandhi began experimenting with language to describe this method of struggle when he was in South Africa, and explained his challenges with terminology as follows: "The resistance to authority in South Africa was well advanced before I got the essay of [US writer Henry David] Thoreau on civil disobedience. But the movement [in South Africa] was then known as passive resistance. As it was incomplete, I had coined the word *satyagraha* for the Gujarati readers. When I saw the title of Thoreau's great essay, I began the use of the phrase [civil disobedience] to explain our struggle to the English readers. But I found that even civil disobedience failed to convey the full meaning of the struggle. I therefore adopted the phrase 'civil resistance.'" Jack, Homer (ed.), *The Wit and Wisdom of Gandhi*. (Mineola, NY: Dover Publications, Inc.), 1979, p. 87-88.

other languages, and thus needs to be created. This is a critically important task for a translator. Civil resistance is a form of political struggle, often driven by strategic thinking. An incorrect translation of this and related terms—for example translating "nonviolent action" as "pacifism" or moral "nonviolence"—can misrepresent the field and in some cases reduce people's receptivity to it. Other translators may incorrectly use the term "protest" as a synonym for "civil resistance," even though "protest" is a single tactic and "civil resistance" is a method of struggle that includes hundreds of diverse tactics. Another key term that may be mistranslated is the term "movement," which could incorrectly be described by using the word "crowd."

Such inaccurate choices of terminology can have real-world implications. Choosing words that do not reflect accurate meanings can prevent ideas from being understood and shared. It can hinder the effective training of activists, and influence people's choices about if and how to mobilize. Therefore, great care must be taken to convey meaning and construct new terms in a language where no such terms currently exist.

2. **In some cases, the English terminology remains unclear.**

A second reason why translating in this field is challenging is that English-language terminology is not always clear. Even while new English-language terms have been created to more accurately describe civil resistance, there are still disagreements among practitioners, teachers, and scholars about their exact meaning. The term "nonviolence" for example, has at least three different definitions, which can contradict each other in some cases.[iii]

This heterogeneity is due in part to the fact that much of the

---

[iii] This is why we do not recommend using the term "nonviolence" as a synonym for "nonviolent action," "civil resistance," or related terms, but we nonetheless include it in this glossary because it is used in the literature in this field, so translators should understand all of the different potential meanings.

practice and terminology of civil resistance developed in a decentralized way. Every movement and campaign adds to the thinking and understanding of this field. Simultaneously, scholars continue to study and deepen their analysis. Terms emerge and their usage changes depending on cultural context and evolving theories.

The scholar Gene Sharp recognized early in his work that a lack of clear terminology and concepts made it challenging to systematically study and communicate about civil resistance. As such, Sharp sought to standardize and specifically define many terms in this field. Some of his terminology remains in common usage today and some continues to evolve. New terms have also been created by other scholars and practitioners. As a relatively young field of study, harmonization of terms remains limited.

3. **The concepts behind civil resistance often contradict popular understandings of power, violence, and conflict.**

An additional consideration for translators is the fact that civil resistance challenges most commonly held understandings about power, violence, and conflict. Most political, economic, and educational systems—as well as culture, entertainment, and news media—emphasize a view of power that derives from wealth, status, and capacity for violent coercion. The thought that coercive power can come from ordinary people engaging in collective nonviolent action, and that oppression can be overcome through nonviolent means, runs against most popular assumptions.

For example, in English, the term "power" often refers to the capacity to influence and coerce through physical force, official status, or wealth. However, such a view of power cannot explain how ordinary people using nonviolent action triumph over rulers who seem to have all the advantages with regards to weapons and material resources. Thus, explaining civil resistance challenges assumptions about the concept and meaning of the word "power."

Similarly, the term "force" in political science and popular media is often used as a synonym for violence. Yet, another kind of powerful and coercive "force" can be wielded through organized, disciplined, and strategic civil resistance.

The term "conflict" is also often tied to ideas of violence, and the idea of waging aggressive nonviolent conflict is an unfamiliar concept to many.

Because these beliefs and views surrounding "power," "conflict," and "violence" can be reflected in a given language, translators in the field of civil resistance often encounter an additional difficulty with these terms. The content that they are translating may directly or indirectly challenge popular understandings and socialization about how and why things work in society.

About this Glossary

Our primary goal with this glossary is to make translating easier and to make translations as accurate as possible. Here are some notes about our thinking as we developed it:

- **CHOICE OF TERMS TO INCLUDE**

We had two criteria for including terms in this glossary:

1. The term commonly appears in civil resistance literature, including articles, books and training manuals.

2. The term has a particular specialized meaning or concept behind it related to the field of civil resistance, and this special meaning or concept may not be found in a standard English dictionary.

There are other relevant terms that we did not include, either because they are rarely used or because they have no specialized meaning for this field. However, we may have also inadvertently left out various terms that should be in this glossary, and we welcome feedback and questions about adding new terms as well as clarifying definitions of included terms. In subsequent editions, we may add, subtract, or modify terms and definitions, based on feedback from translators and reviewers, as well as the evolution of this field.

■ DEFINITIONS AND COMMENTARY

In developing definitions, we aimed to document the diverse uses and meanings of key terms. In cases where English-language terminology is confusing and ambiguous, we explain the various meanings of a particular term, and then provide guidance via commentary about how translators can navigate through these multiple definitions.[iv]

In some of our definitions, we focus predominantly on the civil resistance connotation of a term, and exclude more standard English definitions. However, it is always possible that in a given circumstance a writer is using a term as a standard dictionary defines it, rather than as a specialized civil resistance term. Therefore, this glossary is meant as a primary source of definitions for translators in this field, but there will likely be instances in the translation process where it will also be important to consult a standard English dictionary as a reference.

[iv] Early on in the writing process, we faced a key choice about how to approach this task: We could try to base definitions on our own opinions of proper usage, or we could instead focus on mapping out the territory of how others use the terms in this evolving field. Because our goal is to help translators, we chose to document how others use these terms, rather than leading with our views about preferred definitions.

■ **FORMAT FOR ENTRIES**

Each entry includes:

- **Part of speech:** These include "noun," "verb," "adjective," etc. In some cases, multiple forms of a term are included as separate entries, i.e., "campaign" (noun) and "campaign" (verb).

- **Definition:** There is at least one definition (related to the field of civil resistance) for each term. In cases where the conventional and civil resistance definitions are similar, the "Commentary" section provides an explanation of why the term was included in the glossary and has special meaning in the civil resistance context.

  Please note that in some cases, there are up to three definitions of a single English term, depending on context. In such cases, several translations of a particular term may be necessary to reflect the different definitions.

- **Commentary:** Additional notes on a term's origin, uses, relationship with other terms, and evolution of meaning.

- **Usage in a sentence:** Most terms feature at least two quotes from civil resistance literature to illustrate and clarify their usage and meaning.

- **Related terms:** A short list of directly related terms. Terms in bold in this section have their own entry in the glossary.

Concluding Thoughts

We hope this glossary is helpful to all those interested in the field of civil resistance. If you are reading this glossary as a translator, we also would like to thank you for taking on this important task.

We welcome your feedback, comments, and questions at: **icnc@nonviolent-conflict.org**

Recommended Initial Readings Before Translating

If you are new to the subject of civil resistance, we encourage you to read the following articles and chapters to get a better sense of this growing field. You will find the full list of available English-language literature and a large collection of translated works in the ICNC online **Resource Library** for further reference.

1. **"The trifecta of civil resistance: Unity, planning, discipline"** by Hardy Merriman, *openDemocracy.net* (online), November 19, 2010.

2. **"How the world is proving Martin Luther King right about nonviolence"** by Erica Chenoweth and Maria Stephan, *Washington Post*, January 18, 2016.

3. **"Civil Resistance: A First Look"** International Center on Nonviolent Conflict, 2010.

4. **"Nonviolent Action and Its Misconceptions: Insights for Social Scientists"** by Kurt Schock, *Political Science & Politics*, October 2003.

Existing Translations of Key Terms

We are happy to share that as of January 2021 many of the terms contained in this glossary have been translated into over thirty languages and dialects. For more information, see the "Translations of Key Terms" section on page 156.

Other References and Sources

For any confusing English-language term encountered in civil resistance literature that is not included in this glossary, below are some other references and sources for further reading, including other relevant glossaries and dictionaries:

- ***Sharp's Dictionary of Power and Struggle: Language of Civil Resistance in Conflicts***, by Gene Sharp, New York: Oxford University Press, 2012.

    Includes over 1,000 entries, an essay on power and realism, two case studies, as well as the list of 198 methods of nonviolent action.

- ***A Glossary of Terms and Concepts in Peace and Conflict Studies***, by Christopher Miller and Mary King, San José, Costa Rica: University for Peace, 2005.

    Includes 81 terms related to peace and conflict studies, offering detailed definitions and descriptions with the occasional quote.

- ***Dictionnaire de la non-violence***, by Jean-Marie Muller, Paris: Éditions du Relié, 2014.

    Includes over 150 terms defined and discussed via a short essay. In French only.

Some teaching manuals and handbooks on strategic nonviolent action also include a short glossary or dictionary, such as:

- ***CANVAS Core Curriculum: A Guide to Effective Nonviolent Struggle***, by Srjda Popovic, Slobodan Djinovic, Ivan Milivojevic, Hardy Merriman and Ivan Marovic, Centre for Applied Nonviolent Action and Strategies, 2007.

    Includes a brief "Glossary of Important Terms in Nonviolent Struggle."

- ***The Handbook for Nonviolent Campaigns, Second Edition*** Gárate, Javier, Subhash Kattel, Christine Schweitzer, and Joanne Sheehan (eds.), London: War Resisters' International, 2014.

    Includes a short glossary of about 20 terms.

Key Terms

in the Study and Translation of Civil Resistance

1. **ACCOMMODATE** (as a result of civil resistance)
2. **ACCOMMODATION** (as a result of civil resistance)
3. **ACCOUNTABILITY**
4. **ACTIVIST**
5. **ADVERSARY**
6. **AGENCY** (human agency)
7. **AGENT PROVOCATEUR** (in the context of civil resistance)
8. **ALLY** (verb)
9. **ALLY** (noun)
10. **ALTERNATIVE INSTITUTION**
11. **AUTHORITARIAN RULE**
12. **AUTHORITY**
13. **BACKFIRE** (verb)
14. **BACKFIRE** (noun)
15. **BACKLASH**
16. **BACKSLIDING, DEMOCRATIC** (noun)
17. **BLOCKADE** (associated with civil resistance) (verb)
18. **BLOCKADE** (associated with civil resistance) (noun)
19. **BOYCOTT** (verb)
20. **BOYCOTT** (noun)
21. **CAMPAIGN** (verb)
22. **CAMPAIGN** (noun)
23. **CAPACITY** (in the context of civil resistance)
24. **CIVIL DISOBEDIENCE**
25. **CIVIL RESISTANCE**
26. **CIVIL SOCIETY**
27. **CIVILIAN-BASED DEFENSE**
28. **COALITION**
29. **COMMISSION, ACT OF OR TACTIC OF**
30. **CONCENTRATION, TACTIC OF**
31. **CONDITIONS** (see "structural conditions")
32. **CONFLICT** (noun)
33. **CONSENT** (political) (verb)
34. **CONSENT** (political) (noun)
35. **CONSTRUCTIVE PROGRAMME** (or "constructive program")
36. **CONVERSION** (as a result of civil resistance)
37. **COUP D'ÉTAT** (or "coup")
38. **CRACK DOWN** (verb)
39. **CRACKDOWN** (noun)
40. **DEFECT** (associated with civil resistance) (verb)
41. **DEFECTION**
42. **DEMOCRATIC BACKSLIDING** (noun) (see "backsliding, democratic")
43. **DEMONSTRATION** (associated with civil resistance)
44. **DICTATORSHIP**
45. **DILEMMA ACTION**
46. **DIRECT ACTION**
47. **DISINTEGRATION** (as a result of civil resistance)
48. **DISPERSION, TACTIC OF**
49. **DISRUPT**
50. **DISRUPTION**
51. **DISSENT** (noun)
52. **DISSIDENT**
53. **DYNAMICS** (of civil resistance)
54. **EMPOWER**

55. **EMPOWERMENT**
56. **ESCALATE** (in a conflict)
57. **ESCALATION** (in a conflict)
58. **EXTERNAL ACTOR**
59. **EXTERNAL SUPPORT**
60. **FAILURE** (associated with civil resistance)
61. **FLANK, VIOLENT** (see "violent flank")
62. **FRAME** (in communication) (verb)
63. **FRAME** (in communication) (noun)
64. **FREEDOM** (political)
65. **FREEDOM OF ASSEMBLY**
66. **FREEDOM OF ASSOCIATION**
67. **FREEDOM OF SPEECH** (or "freedom of expression")
68. **GOAL**
69. **GRAND STRATEGY**
70. **GRASSROOTS** (adjective)
71. **GRASSROOTS** (plural noun)
72. **GRIEVANCE**
73. **HUMAN RIGHTS DEFENDER** (or "HRD")
74. **INSURRECTION, UNARMED**
75. **LEADERSHIP**
76. **LEGITIMACY**
77. **LOYALTY SHIFT**
78. **MARCH** (noun)
79. **MASS DEMONSTRATION**
80. **MECHANISMS OF CHANGE**
81. **METHODS OF NONVIOLENT ACTION**
82. **MOBILIZATION**
83. **MOBILIZE**
84. **MOVEMENT**
85. **NONCOOPERATION**
86. **NONGOVERNMENTAL ORGANIZATION** (or "NGO")
87. **NON-STATE ACTOR** (or "nonstate actor")
88. **NONVIOLENCE**
89. **NONVIOLENCE, PRAGMATIC**
90. **NONVIOLENCE, PRINCIPLED**
91. **NONVIOLENT** (or "non-violent")
92. **NONVIOLENT ACTION**
93. **NONVIOLENT COERCION**
94. **NONVIOLENT CONFLICT**
95. **NONVIOLENT DIRECT ACTION**
96. **NONVIOLENT DISCIPLINE**
97. **NONVIOLENT INTERVENTION**
98. **NONVIOLENT STRUGGLE**
99. **OBEDIENCE**
100. **OBEY**
101. **OBJECTIVE** (noun)
102. **OMISSION, ACT OF OR TACTIC OF**
103. **OPPONENT**
104. **OPPOSITION GROUP**
105. **ORGANIZER** (in the context of civil resistance)
106. **PARALLEL INSTITUTION**
107. **PEOPLE POWER**
108. **PILLARS OF SUPPORT**
109. **PLAN** (verb)
110. **PLAN** (noun)
111. **POLITICAL DEFIANCE**
112. **POLITICAL JIU-JITSU**

KEY TERMS   **13**

113. **POLITICAL NONCOOPERATION**
114. **POLITICAL POWER**
115. **POLITICAL SPACE**
116. **POLITICAL TRANSITION** (see "transition, political")
117. **POWER** (noun)
118. **POWERHOLDER** (or "power holder" or "power-holder")
119. **PRAGMATIC NONVIOLENCE** (see "nonviolence, pragmatic")
120. **PRINCIPLED NONVIOLENCE** (see "nonviolence, principled")
121. **PROTEST** (verb)
122. **PROTEST** (noun)
123. **RALLY** (noun)
124. **REPRESS** (in the context of civil resistance)
125. **REPRESSION** (in the context of civil resistance)
126. **RESILIENCE**
127. **REVOLUTION** (social, political, or economic)
128. **SANCTIONS** (plural noun)
129. **SELF-DETERMINATION**
130. **SELF-ORGANIZE** (verb)
131. **SELF-ORGANIZATION**
132. **SELF-RELIANCE**
133. **SELF-RULE**
134. **SEMI-AUTHORITARIAN**
135. **SIT-IN** (noun)
136. **SKILLS** (in the context of civil resistance)
137. **SOURCES OF POWER**
138. **STRATEGIC NONVIOLENT STRUGGLE**
139. **STRATEGIC PLAN**
140. **STRATEGIZE**
141. **STRATEGY**
142. **STRIKE** (associated with civil resistance) (verb)
143. **STRIKE** (associated with civil resistance) (noun)
144. **STRUCTURAL CONDITIONS**
145. **SUCCESS** (associated with civil resistance)
146. **TACTIC**
147. **TACTICAL INNOVATION**
148. **TACTICAL SEQUENCING** (or "sequencing of tactics") (noun)
149. **TACTIC OF CONCENTRATION** (see "concentration, tactic of")
150. **TACTIC OF DISPERSION** (see "dispersion, tactic of")
151. **THIRD PARTY** (or "third-party") (noun)
152. **TRAIN** (verb)
153. **TRAINING** (noun)
154. **TRANSITION, POLITICAL**
155. **UNARMED INSURRECTION** (see "insurrection, unarmed")
156. **UNITE**
157. **UNITY**
158. **UPRISING**
159. **VIOLENCE**
160. **VIOLENT FLANK**
161. **VISION** (of a civil resistance movement)
162. **WALK OUT** (verb)
163. **WALK-OUT** (or "walkout") (noun)

Glossary

Definitions, Commentary, Usage and Related Terms

Note: Related Terms that are **bolded** are defined in this glossary. Related terms that are not bolded are not defined in this glossary.

1   ACCOMMODATE
(as a result of civil resistance)

VERB

The act of engaging in accommodation to meet some or all of the demands of a group waging civil resistance.

■ COMMENTARY

See the commentary for the term **accommodation** (p. 17).

Also, note that this verb may have some variations in the way it is used in the literature, for example:

*"The dilemma facing the government was either to clamp down with all the coercive power necessary in order to eradicate the dissidence, which it had all the instruments to do, or to **accommodate** itself to the fact that it was progressively losing control over a renascent civil society."*[1]

In this instance, "accommodate" means to accept a fact or reality, rather than to accept a particular demand of a movement.

■ USAGE IN A SENTENCE

*"Mid-level military officers may be more likely to **accommodate** the movement than those of higher positions."*[2]

*"Often the opponent or target group decides to **accommodate** the nonviolent protagonists, because the cost of continued struggle is too high or it would be best to cut its losses."*[3]

■ RELATED TERMS

compromise, negotiate, settle

2   ACCOMMODATION
(as a result of civil resistance)

NOUN

The granting of concessions or compromises by a powerholder in response to pressure from civil resistance. Accommodation occurs when powerholders have neither changed their views nor been nonviolently coerced, but have concluded that granting certain demands of nonviolent resisters and/or coming to compromise settlement is desirable.[4]

■ **COMMENTARY**

Accommodation is one of the three "mechanisms of change" of civil resistance (the other mechanisms are "conversion" and "nonviolent coercion") that were first developed by the activist and educator George Lakey.[5] These mechanisms appear frequently in the writings of the scholar Gene Sharp, who also added a fourth mechanism of change called "disintegration."

■ **USAGE IN A SENTENCE**

*"Some segments of the Israeli public became converted to the resisters' cause, mobilizing into an active peace movement, and the regime was enticed into adopting **accommodation** strategies, exemplified by the Oslo peace process and 1993 Washington declaration recognising the Palestinian right to statehood."*[6]

*"**Accommodation** occurs in almost all labor strike settlements. The final agreed working conditions and wages are usually somewhere between the originally stated objectives of the two sides."*[7]

*"**Accommodation** occurs when the opponent does a cost-benefit analysis and arrives at the conclusion that a compromise settlement is a more favorable option than facing continued resistance."*[8]

■ **RELATED TERMS**

compromise, **mechanisms of change**, negotiation, settlement

---

3 ACCOUNTABILITY

NOUN

The concept that individuals, public officials, and institutions should be held responsible for their actions.[9]

■ **COMMENTARY**

There are various forms of accountability.

For example, "political accountability" means the responsibility or obligation of government officials to act in the best interests of society or face consequences for not doing so. "Legal accountability" concerns the mechanisms by which public officials can be held liable for actions that go against established rules and principles.[10]

■ **USAGE IN A SENTENCE**

"[The Citizens Alliance for the General Elections campaign in South Korea] reclaimed their power to demand of political parties worthier representatives and defeat those candidates who

had not acted in the interests of the people they were obligated to serve. In doing so... [they] exacted **accountability** from both the political establishment and the individuals within that corrupt system."[11]

"Once the forum begins, local activists present the results of their investigations, ...officials are questioned, and citizens demand **accountability** of them."[12]

■ **RELATED TERMS**
liability, responsibility

4 ACTIVIST

NOUN

A person who diligently and repeatedly tries to achieve some social, economic, or political objective, especially by creating pressure through protest, organizing other people, voicing public dissent, and/or engaging in acts of resistance.[13]

■ **COMMENTARY**
The term "organizer" and the term "activist" are sometimes used interchangeably in civil resistance literature. However, the term "organizer" emphasizes planning and recruiting others to join a movement, while the term "activist" places emphasis on direct action-taking as part of a movement.

Activists also sometimes play the role of, or are referred to as, human rights defenders. However, these terms are not synonymous. The latter emphasizes work related to the protection or implementation of human rights. See the commentary for the term **human rights defender** (p. 77).

■ **USAGE IN A SENTENCE**
"Otpor **activists**, together with the formal political opposition... began planning to use the election to orchestrate [Serbian President] Milosevic's ouster. They expected that Milosevic would attempt to steal the election through rigging, but planned to expose the fraud through nationwide election monitoring, and to enforce the result through calling on people to protest until Milosevic stepped down."[14]

"Female **activists** in Syria continued to participate in demonstrations even as armed conflict took hold, with many shifting to the work of empowering civil society when protesting became too dangerous. Out of this emerged the Syrian Women's Initiative for Peace and Democracy (SWIPD), a network of women's civil society organizations that has strongly advocated for a peaceful resolution to the conflict, and for women's involvement at the negotiating table for the last three years."[15]

■ **RELATED TERMS**
actionist, **dissident, human rights defender (HRD)**, **organizer**

5 ADVERSARY

NOUN

See the term **opponent** (p. 106).

6 AGENCY
(human agency)

NOUN

The capacity of individuals to make their own free choices, to act independently, and to influence change.

■ **COMMENTARY**

The term "agency" tends to be used in academic literature, particularly in social science. Its origin is from the medieval Latin "*agentia*," which means "doing."

There are debates in the field of civil resistance about the role of agency (also sometimes referred to as "skills" or "strategic choice") versus the role of structural conditions (also sometimes referred to as "conditions" or "structures") in determining the emergence and outcomes of civil resistance movements. Examples of agency include factors that a movement can control, such as its message, strategy, and tactical choices. Examples of structural conditions include factors in a movement's environment (which the movement cannot easily control in the short-term), such as a country's economy, political system, education and literacy levels, demographics, geography, level of internet usage, level of corruption, and many other factors.

The noun form "agent" is a person or group that is exercising their agency.

■ **USAGE IN A SENTENCE**

*"Across countries, societies, [and] contexts... citizens demonstrated that they have **agency** and the capacity to wield power through strategic nonviolent actions...."* [16]

*"Nonviolent movements have become a new form of human **agency**."* [17]

*"... successful civil resistance relies on the decisive **agency** of local people, not foreign forces."* [18]

■ **RELATED TERMS**
action, agent, free choice

7 AGENT PROVOCATEUR
(in the context of civil resistance)

NOUN

A person who joins, or pretends to be part of, a nonviolent campaign or movement and deliberately seeks to sabotage, reduce the effectiveness of, or sow divisions within that campaign or movement, often by encouraging or committing violent acts.

■ **COMMENTARY**

Agents provocateurs may be independent individuals seeking to advance their own agenda or they may be employed and paid by a movement's opponent. [19]

Their aim is to undermine a particular nonviolent action (for example by disrupting an otherwise nonviolent demonstration), to create conflict within a nonviolent movement, to divert a movement's resources (time, material, people) towards unstrategic ends, and/or to "give the movement a violent image in an attempt to alienate public support, justify repression, or induce the movement to shift fully to violent means." [20]

This term comes directly from French and as such, note the plural form is *agents provocateurs*. As it is a foreign word in English, it is often italicized.

■ **USAGE IN A SENTENCE**

*"One Special Branch Officer and one policeman who were later interviewed indicated that those who torched the police station were more likely hired as **agents provocateurs** to create a pretext for the government to use violence."* [21]

*"In some other cases, including labor strikes, **agents provocateurs** employed by the opponents have been used to provoke violence."* [22]

■ **RELATED TERMS**
agitator, infiltrator, informant, provocateur, saboteur, spoiler

8 ALLY

VERB

The act of choosing to align with and support a person, group, institution, movement, or cause.

■ **USAGE IN A SENTENCE**
*"Church officials [in the Philippines] actively brought together noncommunist opposition politicians and members of the business community. The more progressive elements of the church **allied** with grassroots groups and organized Basic Christian Communities in the rural areas, strengthening the church-based mobilization effort and drawing away potential recruits from the guerrilla resistance."* [23]

*"Because of a recent incident of police brutality, the police had the moral low ground. It was easy for us to **ally** with mass media and gain attention for our campaign."* [24]

■ **RELATED TERMS**
align, coalition building

9 ALLY

NOUN

A person, group, or institution that is working together with another person, group, or institution for mutual benefit or to achieve some common purpose.

■ **COMMENTARY**
Many civil resistance movements—and their opponents—have allies, and there are variations of this term that may be used to describe them.

For example, strategic planners sometimes draw a distinction between "active allies" and "passive allies." "Active allies" actively support one side of a conflict. "Passive allies" are sympathetic to the goals of one side of a conflict but are not actively engaged in support. For a civil resistance movement, a key challenge is shifting a movement's passive allies into active allies.[25]

Another example of variation in this term is that some people may refer to the importance of "international allies" that reside outside of the country where the conflict is taking place.

Some people use the term "external ally" to refer to an ally that is not directly impacted by (or not directly part of) the conflict. Such an external ally can be international (for example, a foreign government or an international NGO), or domestic (for example, a local campaign in a specific city may seek external allies in other cities around the country).

Sometimes allies formalize their cooperation by becoming an alliance.

■ **USAGE IN A SENTENCE**

*"A nonviolent posture is more likely to attract potential **allies** abroad and gain the support of groups within the occupier's society while a violent response is more likely to dismay international state and nonstate actors and solidify the support of the occupier's society for repressive tactics against the occupied population."* [26]

*"Foreign election monitors can be valuable **allies** in the effort to assure accurate election results, especially if they came from countries with experience in successful transitions to democracy."*[27]

■ **RELATED TERMS**

alliance, **coalition**, spectrum of allies (strategic planning tool used in civil resistance)

10 ALTERNATIVE INSTITUTION

NOUN

An unofficial (and sometimes informal) social, political, or economic institution that is created by people in a nonviolent campaign or movement.

■ **COMMENTARY**

Building alternative institutions is a tactic of civil resistance. It increases the capacity and self-reliance of a nonviolent movement, and it may also undermine popular support for institutions that are controlled by the movement's opponent.

The function of alternative institutions may be to:

- meet social, economic, or political needs of a population that may otherwise not be served by existing official institutions;
- replace or substitute for existing official institutions that are corrupt, ineffective, or harmful (alternative institutions with this function are sometimes referred to as "parallel institutions"); or
- directly support the execution of a tactic (e.g., striking workers may need to establish a strike fund and management committee to support their labor strike).

Examples of these kinds of institutions include alternative: schools, business enterprises, financial management bodies, media outlets, communication systems, dispute resolution bodies, governing bodies, clubs, committees established to support and organize tactics, and other entities.

■ **USAGE IN A SENTENCE**

"Movement activists construct **alternative institutions** or autonomous 'spaces' in which opposition... strategies can be disseminated."[28]

"... self-organized **alternative institutions**... created an organic link between ordinary life and work on one hand and resistance on the other."[29]

■ **RELATED TERMS**
constructive programme, parallel government, **parallel institution**

---

11   AUTHORITARIAN RULE

NOUN

A government in which the ruler, ruling party, or elites govern in a way that enables them to exercise their decisions without institutional restraint, and without regard for popular will. Under authoritarian rule, opposition to the government is repressed, often through violence, and a population's human rights are often violated.

■ **COMMENTARY**

The terms "authoritarian rule" and "dictatorship" are closely related and sometimes used as synonyms. Similarly, the head of an authoritarian government may sometimes be called an "authoritarian" and sometimes be called a "dictator."

When a political system is partially authoritarian, it may be referred to as "semi-authoritarian." See also the commentary for the term **semi-authoritarian** (p. 130).

■ USAGE IN A SENTENCE

*"Despite this lack of political space [in Burma], a political opposition calling for an end to **authoritarian rule** developed after the military suppressed mass demonstrations in 1988."* [30]

*"The [1991 Moscow] coup has been defeated. Mass public defiance and disobedience in the military thwarted the hard-liners' attempt to return to **authoritarian rule**."* [31]

■ RELATED TERMS

authoritarianism, despotic rule, **dictatorship**, **semi-authoritarian**, totalitarianism, tyranny

---

12 AUTHORITY

NOUN

The perception that some individuals' or groups' judgments, decisions, and recommendations should be obeyed and accepted as right, appropriate, and/or legitimate.

■ COMMENTARY

Authority is an important source of power for governments as well as for movements because it influences the willingness of people to obey orders.

Authority can be formal and informal.

"Formal authority" may be bestowed by institutions (such as a government, religious body, school, professional association, military organization, or resistance organization) or individuals (such as president, general, chief executive) that possess authority. For example, an institution may give an individual an official position, office, title, or other honor. That person may thereby gain the perceived right to decide certain matters that may not have been granted on the sole basis of actual qualities and merit.[32]

"Informal authority" involves perceiving authority in persons or groups based on their attributes (such as superior knowledge, insight, experience, wisdom, reputation, or prestige), even if they have no formal authority (i.e., title or connection with a particular institution). For example, in some cultures, people may be more likely to listen to elders because informal authority is conveyed upon them. Such perceived superiority may or may not reflect objective reality.

Often, when writers use the term "authority," they do not state clearly whether they are referring to the formal or informal meaning (or both at the same time) of this term. Translators therefore often will have to use their best judgment to decide.

When a group or individual with authority is using their power, they are sometimes said to be "exercising authority" or "exercising their authority."

The concept of "authority" is closely related to the concept of "legitimacy." See the commentary for the term **legitimacy** (p. 79).

■ USAGE IN A SENTENCE

"**Authority** is necessary for the existence and operation of any regime. All rulers require an acceptance of their authority: their right to rule, command, and be obeyed."[33]

"Otpor identified Milosevic's **authority** as his most important source of power, and also his most vulnerable. Otpor's actions were thus consciously designed simultaneously to bolster the students' moral **authority** among the population at large and to weaken the **authority** of the regime."[34]

■ RELATED TERMS

leadership, legitimacy, political power, power (noun)

---

13   BACKFIRE

VERB

To rebound adversely on the initiator of an action. To have the opposite effect of what is intended.[35]

■ COMMENTARY

See the commentary for the term **backfire** (noun) (p. 27).

■ USAGE IN A SENTENCE

"In 1991, thousands of people joined a funeral procession in Dili, East Timor, using the occasion to peacefully protest against the Indonesian occupation. As the procession entered Santa Cruz cemetery, Indonesian troops suddenly opened fire, killing hundreds of people. Western journalists were present and recorded the massacre. Their testimony and video evidence triggered a huge increase in international support for the East Timorese *liberation movement and laid the basis for independence a decade later. The massacre of peaceful protesters **backfired** on the Indonesian government."* [36]

■ RELATED TERMS
backfire (noun), **backlash, political jiu-jitsu**

---

14   BACKFIRE

NOUN

A situation in which a plan or action rebounds adversely on the initiator and has the opposite effect to what was intended.

■ COMMENTARY

The term "backfire" is most commonly used to describe a situation in which a movement's opponent engages in repression (for example, beating nonviolent protesters) that increases public sympathy for the movement, and undermines the opponent's legitimacy.

The term has been popularized in the field of civil resistance by the scholar Brian Martin, who identified and developed a five-step process through which backfire happens.

The definition of the term "backfire" is very similar to the term "backlash." However, they tend to be used in different circumstances in civil resistance literature. "Backfire" usually refers to instances when repression against a civil resistance movement has a negative impact on the movement's opponent. The term "backlash" tends to refer to a strong negative reaction to either the movement or the movement's opponent.

The definition of the term "backfire" is also similar to the term "political jiu-jitsu," which is often used in the writings of the scholar Gene Sharp.

■ USAGE IN A SENTENCE

*"**Backfire** occurred when the violent repression of unarmed protesters generated widespread public outrage, which in turn decreased the regime's political legitimacy and increased challenger mobilization."* [37]

"... the armed forces—the police, secret security, and the military—play a pivotal role in civil resistance movements. They may arrest or attack protesters, potentially undercutting the movement's

*strength or launching the **backfire** dynamic that can shift the balance of power."* ³⁸

■ **RELATED TERMS**
backfire (verb), **backlash**, **political jiu-jitsu**

---

15 BACKLASH

NOUN

An unintended and undesired negative reaction to certain actions by either side in a conflict.

■ **COMMENTARY**
Often, backlash causes third parties or sections of the population that were previously uninvolved or neutral in a conflict to become more actively involved in supporting one side or another.

Such a reaction is common when previously nonviolent resisters begin to use violence or when a government or opponent of a nonviolent movement uses brutal repression, terrorism, and other violent acts. These acts may be rejected by various persons and groups irrespective of their views on the issues in the conflict. Backlash may also occur as a result of other actions (for example use of particular words, speech, or symbols) that are offensive.³⁹

The definition of the term "backlash" is very similar to the term "backfire." However, they tend to be used in different circumstances in civil resistance literature. The term "backlash" tends to be used to refer to a strong negative reaction to either party in a conflict. The term "backfire" almost always refers to instances when an act of repression against a civil resistance movement hurts the movement's opponent instead. It is rarely used to refer to instances when violence or statements by a movement hurt the movement.

■ **USAGE IN A SENTENCE**
"***Backlash** against violent government actions has often been magnified by word-of-mouth about committed atrocities..., by communication tools such as telegraph and newspapers..., or by the Internet and social media....*" ⁴⁰

"*Government officials at first tried to marginalize and trivialize them by calling them 'las locas,' the madwomen, but they were baffled as to how to suppress this group for fear of a **backlash** among the population.*" ⁴¹

■ **RELATED TERMS**
backfire (noun), **backfire** (verb), **political jiu-jitsu**

---

16 BACKSLIDING, DEMOCRATIC

NOUN

The weakening and/or eliminating of the political institutions and freedoms that underpin a democratic political system. Such a process may happen gradually or quickly, and often takes place when elected public authorities deliberately cause the quality of democracy to decline as a way to force through their political agenda and/or insulate their rule from democratic challenges.

■ **COMMENTARY**

Democratic backsliding is a process of modifying institutions and democratic norms incrementally in ways that systematically concentrate power in the executive branch of government and erode government accountability. This often happens through increasing personal powers of certain actors, curbing protected freedoms (such as freedom of speech and freedom of assembly, frequently with the justification of defending national security), disabling internal checks on power and monitoring mechanisms and impeding the work of civil society watchdogs.

Specific examples may include:

o Passing legislation to strengthen the power of executive government institutions and weaken independent institutions that may oppose the executive.

o Weakening the rights and protections of certain groups (i.e., civil society groups) in society that may challenge executive institutions.

o Strengthening the rights and protections of a leader's political supporters or economic allies.

o Using vested political and institutional powers to their maximum extent in ways that violate long-standing democratic political norms and lead to constitutional crises.

o Seeking to categorically delegitimize democratic opposition, and sometimes persecute this opposition for political reasons

- Appointing personnel—particularly to the judiciary branch—based primarily on loyalty to a ruling party rather than competence and qualifications.
- Using the power of the state to curtail or limit independent media.
- Changing electoral laws, processes, or practices in ways that limit popular participation or equality in voting.
- Disabling monitoring bodies or mechanisms—within government, the private sector, or within civil society—from exercising oversight of political or economic affairs.
- Using rhetoric to deliberately sow divisions in a population and increase polarization.
- Engaging in corruption to accomplish any of the above means.

Democratic backsliding is also known as "democratic decline," "democratic erosion" or "de-democratization."

■ **USAGE IN A SENTENCE**

*Military coups [are]... no longer the autocrat's instrument of choice. It is instead more common to see a steady trickle of institutional erosions. What's more, even highly compromised democracies such as Russia, and now Turkey, maintain a semblance of democratic contestation and electoral process after more than a decade of **democratic backsliding**.* [42]

■ **RELATED TERMS**

democratic decline, democratic erosion, de-democratization, rule of law backsliding

17 BLOCKADE
(associated with civil resistance)

VERB

The act of engaging in a nonviolent blockade.

■ **USAGE IN A SENTENCE**

*"The following day the students **blockaded** the Secretariat, the colonial administrative center for the entire country. It was an audacious action. No group in Burma had ever organized nonviolent direct action on this scale. Each gate had rows of students blocking entry and no government employee could go to work, effectively shutting down the colonial civil administration."* [43]

*"... indigenous communities in the Amazon rainforest **blockaded** access to loggers or miners by physically obstructing roads and vehicles."* [44]

■ **RELATED TERMS**
intervene, obstruct

---

18 BLOCKADE
(associated with civil resistance)

NOUN

A nonviolent action designed to prevent people and goods from accessing a given location.

Blockades may be established by objects (such as parked cars, or boats in the case of a "naval blockade"), construction of structures (such as walls) or a mass of people, who may be sitting, standing, or lying down.

■ **USAGE IN A SENTENCE**

*"A general strike began on 2 October in an effort to nullify [President Slobodan] Milosevic's control over the country; it was at first ineffective in Belgrade, but widely supported in the provinces where several cities were completely shut down because of **blockades** by cars, trucks, buses, and people, as well as closed businesses and schools."* [45]

*"... the [Dosta! ("Enough!")] youth movement became synonymous with grassroots organizing, civic activism, and transcending ethnic and religious divisions. It utilized a diverse range of nonviolent tactics, such as silent marches against corruption, petitions demanding the resignation of crooked local officials, a nonviolent **blockade** of [the capital city] Sarajevo to protest police brutality, cultural activities, and alternative social services."* [46]

■ **RELATED TERMS**
civil disobedience, **nonviolent intervention**, nonviolent obstruction

19 BOYCOTT

VERB

The act of engaging in a boycott.

■ **COMMENTARY**

See the commentary for the term **boycott** (noun) (p. 32).

■ **USAGE IN A SENTENCE**

*"During the 1920-1922 campaign, Indians refused to participate in British-run schools, government offices, and courts. They **boycotted** British cotton imports, instead making their own homespun cloth. Gandhi and his colleagues organized an even larger boycott of British goods during the 1930-1931 salt satyagraha."*[47]

*"Economic forms of noncooperation provided more powerful sanctions. Organized campaigns of nonimportation of British goods imposed an economic cost on the British. Between October 31 and December 8, 1765, most merchants along the eastern seaboard cities **boycotted** British goods."*[48]

■ **RELATED TERMS**

consumer boycott, economic noncooperation, election boycott, **noncooperation**, **political noncooperation**, school boycott, social boycott

20 BOYCOTT

NOUN

A category of methods of nonviolent noncooperation in which a party refuses to continue or to enter into economic, social, or political relationships with another party, in order to influence the behavior of that party.

■ **COMMENTARY**

There are different kinds of boycotts. In a "consumer boycott," consumers refuse to purchase or use the goods of targeted producers. In a "producers boycott," producers refuse to sell to a given party. Similarly, the notion has been extended to various aspects of social and political relationships, such as the ostracism of individuals through a "social boycott," refusal to attend classes in a "school boycott," and refusal to participate in voting procedures in an "election boycott."[49]

■ **USAGE IN A SENTENCE**

"In 1985 the activists declare a **boycott** of white-owned businesses and demand the troops' withdrawal and release of political prisoners. Stores in [the city of] Port Elizabeth lose about one-third of their business, and white owners begin clamoring for officials to meet the boycotters' demands."[50]

"When the day of the [Montgomery, Alabama] bus **boycott** arrived, even the participants were stunned by its near-total effectiveness. Buses drove around empty all day throughout the African American neighborhoods."[51]

■ **RELATED TERMS**

consumer boycott, economic boycott, economic noncooperation, election boycott, **noncooperation**, **political noncooperation**, school boycott, social boycott

21 CAMPAIGN

VERB

To work in an active way toward a particular goal, particularly a political or social one.[52]

■ **COMMENTARY**

See the commentary for the term **campaign** (noun) (p. 34).

■ **USAGE IN A SENTENCE**

"In the rural areas of Southern Province [of Zambia], especially the Plateau Tonga region, small-scale commercial farmers... formed the local leadership in protest politics during the 1930s and 1940s. They aimed at exerting influence on local councils and chiefs and sabotaging government programs by **campaigning** against local participation and cooperation with government officials."[53]

"... it became easy for opposition political parties in East Pakistan to form a United Front (UF), **campaigning** on the promise to make Bangla a national language and a language of instruction in the East Pakistani education system."[54]

■ **RELATED TERMS**

advocate, **mobilize**, rally (verb)

22 CAMPAIGN

NOUN
1. "A series of repetitive, durable... [and] organized events directed at a certain target to achieve a goal."[55]
2. A coordinated series of tactics and operations that are planned on the basis of a broader strategy. Campaign objectives are to be accomplished within a certain timeframe and geography. Campaigns can be waged through civil resistance, military action, electoral competition, or through other means (for example, advertising or marketing).[56] Some campaigns will combine a variety of means (i.e., have an electoral and civil resistance component).

■ COMMENTARY

The noun "campaign" is used in two predominant ways in civil resistance literature.

According to the first (and broader) definition, the term "campaign" is sometimes used as a synonym for the term "movement." It means people organizing over time and taking collective action to achieve one or more goals.

According to the second (and narrower) definition, in the context of civil resistance a "campaign" refers to *a particular phase of a movement* and is used to describe a series of actions to achieve a significant, intermediate objective by that movement. For example, the US Civil Rights Movement had numerous campaigns in different cities at different times during its existence, including the Montgomery Bus Boycott, the Nashville Lunch Counter Sit-Ins.

■ USAGE IN A SENTENCE

*"Unless **campaigns** find ways to mobilize mass participation, disrupt the normal order of things and deprive opponents of their means of maintaining the status quo, even the most righteous causes fall flat."*[57] *(illustrates the first definition)*

*"Not all major changes can be achieved in a single struggle. A series of **campaigns** may be required, with temporary pauses between them."*[58] *(illustrates the second definition)*

■ RELATED TERMS

movement, operation, **strategy**, **tactic**

23 CAPACITY
(in the context of civil resistance)

NOUN

The ability of people, institutions, movements, and/or societies to perform functions, solve problems, and set and achieve objectives.[59]

■ **COMMENTARY**

A movement's "capacity" refers to various capabilities that enable the movement to succeed, for example its ability to engage in strategic planning, take unified action, sustain nonviolent discipline, resist repression, mobilize large numbers of people, execute certain tactics, and communicate its message to wider audiences.

A government's "capacity" refers to various capabilities that enable it to rule, for example its ability to control and allocate material resources, deploy human resources and draw on their skills, commit sanctions, and communicate with society (for example, through the media).

Conducting programs and/or taking other actions that aim to increase the capacity of a particular group are often referred to as "capacity building."

■ **USAGE IN A SENTENCE**

*"...citizen-led movements have increasingly defined the outcome of the most geopolitically significant conflicts and democratic transitions since 1972. Yet policy makers, scholars, journalists, and other interested observers consistently underestimate this **capacity** of ordinary people to undermine tyranny and achieve rights without violence."*[60]

*"When participation in civil resistance diversifies and grows, repression against resisters is often insufficient to restore tranquility and instead becomes more likely to backfire. As disruption continues, cracks also begin to appear within the government and other institutions (i.e., police, military, media and political, bureaucratic, and economic entities) critical to the state. These cracks often lead to defections, and as defections cascade, the core **capacities** that an authoritarian depends on for their rule—control of material resources, human resources, people's skills and knowledge, the information environment, and the **capacity** to commit sanctions—are devastated."*[61]

■ **RELATED TERMS**
ability, capability, strength

24 CIVIL DISOBEDIENCE

NOUN

An active and often public nonviolent violation of particular laws, decrees, regulations, ordinances, military or police commands and other orders. This is usually done in protest of laws or orders which are regarded as immoral, unjust, or tyrannical and with the expectation and acceptance by the perpetrator(s) of the legal consequences of this disobedience.

Sometimes an individual or group may disobey a particular law as a symbol of opposition to wider policies of the government, or the government's rule itself. [62]

■ **COMMENTARY**

Many attribute the modern understanding of the concept of "civil disobedience" to Henry David Thoreau and his 1849 essay "Resistance to Civil Government" (which was re-released four years after his death with the title "Civil Disobedience").[63] In his essay, Thoreau explains why he refused to pay taxes in protest against the US war against Mexico. However, it is notable that the concept of civil disobedience precedes Thoreau's essay.

In its original definition, civil disobedience refers only to the intentional non-obedience/violation of laws and judicial decisions of the civil order. However, the scholar Gene Sharp broadens that definition to include disobedience to military commands.

■ **USAGE IN A SENTENCE**

"In early 1930 the Indian National Congress, led by Mohandas Gandhi, launches a campaign of **civil disobedience** *against British colonial rule...."* [64]

"The [South African] Defiance Campaign, a nationwide campaign of **civil disobedience** *in which people disobeyed segregation rule in public places, was launched in 1952."* [65]

■ **RELATED TERMS**

disobedience, **noncooperation, nonviolent intervention**

25 CIVIL RESISTANCE

NOUN

A technique by which one or more people in a society wage conflict to achieve political, economic, or social objectives without the use or threat of physical violence. Civil resistance consists of:

a. acts of commission, whereby people do things that they are not supposed to do, not expected to do, or are forbidden by law to do (such as protests, symbolic actions, nonviolent blockades and occupations);

b. acts of omission, whereby people refuse to do things that they are supposed to do, are expected to do, or are required by law to do (such as strikes, boycotts, and other forms of noncooperation); or

c. a combination of both acts of commission and acts of omission.[66]

■ COMMENTARY

Civil resistance, by definition, refers to actions that are *outside* of formal or institutional means of making change. This means that civil resistance generally does not include voting in elections or following official procedures for complaint (like filing a lawsuit), both of which are processes established by (state) institutions themselves. However, in practice, many civil resistance movements also engage in institutional means of making change, with the view that both approaches can work together and reinforce each other. In some cases, civil resistance can be necessary to get official institutional methods of change to work effectively.

It is also notable that although civil resistance takes place outside of institutional channels of making change, civil resistance can be organized within institutions themselves. For example, state bureaucrats may engage in a strike or slow down.

One of the reasons why the term civil resistance is sometimes used instead of the terms "nonviolent action" and "nonviolent struggle" is because some people hear the word "nonviolent" and assume that it refers to pacifism or a set of ethical beliefs, rather than a strategic mode of struggle.

Civil resistance can generally be used as a synonym for the terms "nonviolent action," "nonviolent struggle," "nonviolent conflict," "nonviolent resistance," "people power," and "political defiance." The common idea behind these terms is the aim to shift power in society through mass withdrawal of consent and obedience by a population. Civil resistance succeeds by unifying and mobilizing people, sequencing nonviolent tactics to achieve strategic goals, imposing costs on powerholders, and undermining powerholders' sources of power.

When people participate in civil resistance in a collective and organized way, they are often said to be part of a "civil resistance movement," "civil resistance campaign," or "nonviolent struggle."

See also the commentary for the term **nonviolence** (p. 90), to ensure that the terms "civil resistance" and "nonviolence" are not confused.

See also the commentary for the term **violence** (p. 152), to better understand actions that are prohibited under the term "civil resistance."

■ **USAGE IN A SENTENCE**

*"**Civil resistance** occurs when people cannot make progress on fundamental issues of life, liberty, and property solely by conventional politics... or by discourse and mediation. Instead, a popular movement or campaign chooses to battle with nonviolent methods, while the antagonist relies on its institutional authority and, when necessary, its military and police to maintain control."*[67]

*"...**civil resistance** is not only a political and social phenomenon operating under various conditions. It is also a course of human action taken by tens and hundreds of thousands of people, whose skills in engaging in these conflicts have substantial impact on the outcomes."*[68]

■ **RELATED TERMS**

nonviolent action, **nonviolent conflict**, nonviolent resistance, **nonviolent struggle, people power, political defiance**

---

26 CIVIL SOCIETY

NOUN

Groups and organizations (which may be formal or informal) working in the interest of a population, or segments of a population, and operating outside of the governmental and for-profit (business) sectors.

■ **COMMENTARY**

Examples of civil society groups include everything from officially registered nongovernmental organizations (NGOs) to labor and trade unions, religious groups, student groups, economic cooperatives, professional associations, and many other groups that operate formally or informally at the local, regional, or national level independently of the state. Such groups or organizations are sometimes referred to as "civil society organizations" (CSOs).

Civil society generally refers to groups that contribute to civic life and a society's interests and advance democratic values. The existence and strength of civil society is widely viewed as a critical factor in achieving and maintaining freedoms, social justice, and the development and maintenance of a democratic political system. Although it is not inherent in the definition of civil society that civil society groups are nonviolent, in practice the term "civil society" generally does not refer to armed groups.

■ **USAGE IN A SENTENCE**

*"Mass nonviolent mobilization and participation enabled societies to reject foreign dominance and indoctrination while practicing self-governance and building the nucleus of a new **civil society**."* [69]

*"The struggles in Burma and China in the late 1980s were unsuccessful in toppling their states, but they may have set in motion a process of developing oppositional **civil society** that will contribute to political change in the future."* [70]

■ **RELATED TERMS**

civic sector, civil society organization (CSO), **nongovernmental organization (NGO)**, not-for-profit (non-profit) sector

27 CIVILIAN-BASED DEFENSE

NOUN

Nonviolent defense by civilians to deter or defeat foreign military invasions, occupations, and internal usurpations such as coups d'état.

■ **COMMENTARY**

The scholar Gene Sharp, author of several key works on civilian-based defense, states that: "Deterrence and defense are to be accomplished by social, economic, political, and psychological means of struggle. These are used to wage widespread noncooperation and to offer massive public defiance to attacks. The aim is to deny the attackers their desired objectives, and to make impossible the consolidation of foreign rule, a puppet government, or a government of usurpers."[71]

■ **USAGE IN A SENTENCE**

*"The policy of '**civilian-based defense**' has been developed to build on improvised experience with nonviolent struggle against aggression and occupations, such as in the Ruhr in Germany in 1923, Czechoslovakia in 1968-1969, and the Baltic countries in 1990-1991."* [72]

*"The real power of **civilian-based defense** is the threat, or promise, to use the power of civilian society to prevent war and immobilize an occupant, rather than threaten to destroy that society in order to deny it to the enemy."* [73]

- **RELATED TERMS**

civilian defense, nonmilitary defense, nonviolent defense

28 COALITION

NOUN

A group that is formed by different organizations, groups or individuals who agree to act together, usually temporarily, to achieve one or more common objectives.

- **COMMENTARY**

Coalitions are part of many—although not all—civil resistance movements. The formation of coalitions may lead to the formation of a civil resistance movement, or the formation of a civil resistance movement may lead to the formation of coalitions.

Research shows that the level of public participation in a movement is a major factor in movement success.[74] High participation rates lead to more powerful and successful movements. Coalitions can play an important role in helping to coordinate action and mobilize different groups of people to support and participate in a movement.

The process of building coalitions is often referred to as "coalition building."

- **USAGE IN A SENTENCE**

*"The CICAK [Love Indonesia, Love Anti-corruption Commission] campaign demonstrated that an effective division of labor is essential for civic initiatives, particularly ones involving a **coalition** or alliance of multiple groups."* [75]

*"[A] **coalition** of local brokers, market women, and chiefs organized a boycott of European goods and refused to sell cocoa."* [76]

- **RELATED TERMS**

alliance, **ally** (noun), coalition building

29 COMMISSION, ACT OF OR TACTIC OF

NOUN

A civil resistance action in which people do things that they are not supposed to do, not expected to do, or are forbidden by law from doing.[77]

■ **COMMENTARY**

In the field of civil resistance, an act of commission is always intentional. This makes its meaning narrower than in general English usage, where an act of commission could also be unintentional.

Examples of acts of commission include mass demonstrations; nonviolent obstruction, blockades, occupations, or interventions; and symbolic acts of protest.

■ **USAGE IN A SENTENCE**

*"In the Tibetan mindset, only acts of **commission** that are visible and action-oriented—protest demonstrations, marches and vigils, the chanting of slogans, waving the national flag—are worthy of being counted and documented as acts of resistance. This rather narrow conceptualization of nonviolent resistance has been a major obstacle to the comprehensive documentation of civil resistance in Tibet."*[78]

■ **RELATED TERMS**

act of omision, **tactic of omission**, **demonstration**, picketing, **protest** (noun), **rally** (noun), **sit-in** (noun)

30 CONCENTRATION, TACTIC OF

NOUN

An act of civil resistance in which participants or resources are all densely situated in the same place at the same time.

■ **COMMENTARY**

Examples of tactics of concentration include mass demonstrations, sit-ins, marches, and rallies.

Tactics of concentration tend to be public. They can show lack of fear and (when many people are present) strong and popular support for a cause. However, they also tend to be more vulnerable to repression than other tactics (see definition of **tactics of dispersion**, p. 56).

■ **USAGE IN A SENTENCE**

"***Tactics of concentration**, in which a large number of people are concentrated in a public place (e.g., in a protest demonstration), provide a movement with the opportunity to build solidarity, highlight grievances, indicate the extent of dissatisfaction, and, if the state responds with repression, expose the fact that the state is based on violence rather than legitimacy.*"[79]

"*During the Civil Rights movement in America, one of the most well-known campaigns was the March on Washington, when a million people congregated on the National Mall in Washington, DC. This is perhaps the best example of what a **tactic of concentration** looks like.*"[80]

■ **RELATED TERMS**

centralized, high-risk tactic, **march** (noun), **mass demonstration**, occupation of public spaces, **sit-in** (noun)

---

31 CONDITIONS

PLURAL NOUN

See the term **structural conditions** (p. 140).

---

32 CONFLICT

NOUN

A disagreement, argument, incompatibility, or fight between individuals, groups, institutions, or states.[81]

■ **COMMENTARY**

In some languages, the term "conflict" has a strong connotation that violence is involved. It is important when translating the term "conflict" to remember that conflicts can also be waged through nonviolent means.

Some conflicts may be short-term while others may become protracted and stretch on for years. The scholar Gene Sharp notes that "The degree to which… [the conflicting parties'] respective aims are in contention or incompatible may vary. This variation may influence the choices that each side makes regarding how they will attempt to wage and/or resolve the conflict."[82]

■ **USAGE IN A SENTENCE**

*"The greatest misconception about **conflict** is that violence is the ultimate form of power, surpassing other methods of advancing a just cause or defeating injustice."* [83]

*"Nonviolent action is a means for prosecuting a conflict and it should be distinguished from means of **conflict** resolution."* [84]

■ **RELATED TERMS**
nonviolent conflict, struggle

33 CONSENT
(political)

VERB

To freely agree to do something or give permission for something to happen. [85]

To accept, acquiesce, or allow without resistance something that is required, suggested, or requested. Such behavior does not necessarily indicate agreement with the authority's orders, but it does indicate obedience to their order without resistance.

■ **COMMENTARY**

In general, the verb "consent" in English means actively giving permission for or agreeing to a particular action. Consent is indicated by an affirmative statement or action to show agreement with or give permission for something to happen.

However, in civil resistance literature the verb "consent" is often used in a political context and often refers to carrying out orders with an *absence of resistance or defiance*. This is a critical distinction between how the term is generally defined in English (positive agreement with orders), and how the term is used in civil resistance literature (lack of resistance to orders). In this regard, in civil resistance literature the verb "consent" is similar to the verb "obey." It may be that people consent because they agree with orders or it may be that they consent (acquiesce to or accept orders) because they are too afraid to openly defy those orders, for example.

See also the commentary for the term **consent** (political) (noun) (p. 44).

■ **USAGE IN A SENTENCE**

*"In politics, [the use of nonviolent action] is based upon the immutable maxim that government of the people is possible only so long as they **consent** either consciously or unconsciously to be governed."* [86]

*"Realising that **consent** can be given or taken away is an initial step towards understanding that cooperation is not necessarily guaranteed. It can be purposefully and strategically withdrawn."* [87]

*"While consensus implies freedom to decide one's own course of life, it also comes with responsibilities to the collective. The consensus process is based upon listening and respect, and participation by everyone. The goal is to find a decision that is acceptable to all group members, that everyone **consents** to."* [88]

■ **RELATED TERMS**
accept, allow, cooperate, **obey**

---

34 CONSENT
(political)

NOUN

1. Freely given agreement (obtained from an individual or an entity having authority or power) to do something or permission for something to happen.
2. The acquiescence or obedience without resistance to something that is required, suggested, or requested.

■ **COMMENTARY**

The concept of consent is at the heart of civil resistance theory: Much of nonviolent strategy and tactics is about the active or symbolic withdrawal or denial of consent to upset and change established power relationships.

Consent can be given actively, as when someone willingly obeys an order. Or consent can be implied, which generally refers to a lack of resistance or active disagreement to an order or something that is happening. In civil resistance literature, the noun "consent" is often used to refer to "implied consent" (as in the second definition) or the absence of resistance, and thus is often used as a synonym for the word "obedience."

See also the commentary for the term **consent** (political) (verb) (p. 43).

■ **USAGE IN A SENTENCE**

*"[Mohandas Gandhi] taught that the power of social movements is based on their ability to mobilize the populace in a moral struggle in which the people withdraw their **consent** to be governed by those in power, using methods such as noncooperation, defiance, disobedience, refusing benefits, and creating alternatives."* [89]

*"The withdrawal of **consent**, cooperation, and submission will challenge the system as it affects the opponents' sources of power."* [90]

■ **RELATED TERMS**
obedience

---

35 CONSTRUCTIVE PROGRAMME
(or "constructive program")

NOUN

1. **The plan originally developed by Mohandas Gandhi for developing a new social order through voluntary activities, work, and the establishment of new, independent organizations in communities.**
2. **The active development of alternative institutions as part of a nonviolent struggle.**

■ **COMMENTARY**

Gandhi recommended that "constructive programme" should precede, accompany, and follow the use of nonviolent action.[91] He argued that this would help to correct certain social ills while also building up new institutions that would play major roles in an emerging social order.

The term refers particularly to work in the Indian Independence Struggle, but it has also come to refer more broadly to the active development of alternative institutions as part of any nonviolent struggle.

■ **USAGE IN A SENTENCE**

*"For the individual, **constructive programme** meant increased power-from-within through the development of personal identity, self-reliance, and fearlessness. For the community, it meant the creation of a new set of political, social, and economic relations."* [92]

*"Envisioned by Gandhi as the strongest form of satyagraha, the '**constructive programme**' that is part of many civil resistance*

movements (e.g., alternative or parallel media, social services, tax systems, elections, institutions) is another identity-producing dynamic that supports self-transformation at the individual and collective levels."[93]

■ **RELATED TERMS**
alternative institution, parallel government, **parallel institution**

36 CONVERSION
(as a result of civil resistance)

NOUN

A change of attitude by people who had opposed or were previously neutral towards a civil resistance movement, such that they come to accept and/or actively agree with the objectives of the nonviolent group.[94]

■ **COMMENTARY**

Conversion is one of the three "mechanisms of change" (the other mechanisms are "accommodation" and "nonviolent coercion") of civil resistance that were originally identified by the activist and educator George Lakey.[95] These mechanisms appear frequently in the writings of the scholar Gene Sharp, who also added a fourth mechanism of change called "disintegration."

Sharp envisions conversion as something that could happen to a movement's main adversary (i.e., the president of a country), but others have written about conversion as something that can happen to certain groups within the opponent's pillars of support (i.e., certain members of security forces, members of judiciary) which, combined with other mechanisms of change (i.e., accommodation, nonviolent coercion, and disintegration) on other groups and other pillars (i.e., members of the business community, organized labor), can lead to defections and to the movement achieving its goals.

■ **USAGE IN A SENTENCE**

"*You may rely on some mechanisms, such as **conversion** or accommodation, as you build up strength in the earlier phases of your movement, and only aim for coercion or disintegration in later phases.*"[96]

"***Conversion** is commonly (mis)understood as the only way or the main way in which nonviolent action produces political change. In reality, however, it is the least likely mechanism of change.*"[97]

■ **RELATED TERMS**

accommodation, **defection**, **disintegration**, **loyalty shift**, **mechanisms of change**, **nonviolent coercion**, persuasion

---

37   COUP D'ÉTAT
(or "coup")

NOUN

A rapid seizure of physical and political control of the state apparatus by illegal action of a conspiratorial group backed by the threat or use of violence.

■ **COMMENTARY**

Contrary to a revolution or popular uprising that mobilizes the masses, a coup d'état is instigated and implemented by a limited number of people, although coups sometimes follow major public unrest or nonviolent movements challenging an unpopular ruler.

When the coup is launched by the military, it is sometimes referred to as a "military coup." Coups may also be launched by the leader of a country (which is sometimes referred to as a "self-coup") when the leader overturns Constitutional rule (for example, by declaring a "state of emergency") and takes over control of the state while remaining the leader.

Coup d'état is an expression of French origin (literally "a blow to the state"), first used to describe the seizure of power in France by Napoleon in 1799. The English usage of this term dropped the original spelling with the uppercase E in "coup d'État."

Note the plural form in English is "coups d'état" or simply "coups."

■ **USAGE IN A SENTENCE**

"***Coup(s) d'état*** *have taken place in dozens of countries in nearly every region of the world in recent decades, including Thailand, Burma, the Philippines, Brazil, Czechoslovakia, Ghana, Liberia, Chile, Fiji, Greece, Libya, Laos, Guatemala, Argentina, Grenada, Poland, and the Soviet Union.*"[98]

"*In August 1991, a group of plotters in the former Soviet Union attempted a* ***coup d'état*** *against the government of Mikhail Gorbachev. Massive nonviolent action by the Russian populace defeated the coup. Russian activists formed the group 'Living Ring,' its name based on the large numbers of people who 'ringed' one of Moscow's main government buildings, putting their bodies between armed troops and the legitimate government.*"[99]

■ **RELATED TERMS**
democratic backsliding, overthrow, putsch, usurpation

---

38 CRACK DOWN

VERB

The act of engaging in severe measures (usually by an authority) to stop or discourage people or behavior that is considered undesirable or illegal.

■ **COMMENTARY**
Note that the verb form of this term is two words ("crack down") whereas the noun form is one word ("crackdown").

■ **USAGE IN A SENTENCE**
*"One common scenario leading to loyalty shifts is when the regime violently **cracks down** on a popular nonviolent campaign with mass civilian participation."*[100]

*"By the start of the school year, the PMS [Polish Motherland Schools] boasted 680 registered schools and 70,000 enrolled students. Soon these numbers increased to almost 800 schools and nearly 120,000 pupils, and the next year a further 450 private schools requested registration. Then, the Russian government **cracked down** and closed the PMS themselves."*[101]

■ **RELATED TERMS**
martial law, **repress**

---

39 CRACKDOWN

NOUN

Severe measures (usually by an authority) to stop or discourage people or behavior that is considered undesirable or illegal.

■ **COMMENTARY**
Note that the noun form of this term is one word ("crackdown") whereas the verb form is two words ("crack down").

■ **USAGE IN A SENTENCE**
*"The brutal **crackdown** on both Islamist and secular oppositionists by the US-backed Egyptian military junta has taken on a bizarre twist: using government-controlled media to promote*

long-discredited conspiracy theories originally put forward by ultra-left fringe groups."[102]

*"Condemning **crackdowns** can include exposing violations of international or regional conventions signed by aid-recipient governments, and developing joint statements and actions among like-minded governments."*[103]

■ **RELATED TERMS**
repression, state violence, **violence**

40 DEFECT
(associated with civil resistance)

VERB

The act of abandoning one's allegiance or duty, possibly in favor of an opposing one.

■ **COMMENTARY**

People may defect publicly, as when a person openly begins to defy orders, or privately, as when a person subtly or anonymously begins to disobey orders or deliberately executes orders slowly or inefficiently.

See also the commentary for the term **defection** (p. 50).

■ **USAGE IN A SENTENCE**

*"In the final days of Yanukovych in Kyiv, thirty-six members of his ruling Party of Regions (a number that grew to seventy) decided to **defect** and join the parliamentary opposition in Verkhovna Rada, to vote for the law that ordered the withdrawal of security forces from the streets of Kyiv and their return to garrisons."*[104]

*"We find that, in general, security forces tend to **defect** much more often when they face nonviolent campaigns (as compared to armed uprisings), particularly as the numbers rise."*[105]

■ **RELATED TERMS**
disobedience, **loyalty shift**

41 DEFECTION

NOUN
Conscious abandonment of allegiance or duty (as to a person, cause, or doctrine), possibly in favor of an opposing one.

■ **COMMENTARY**

Defections are an important factor in movement success. Sustained nonviolent resistance tends to lead to defections among a movement's opponent, whereby the opponent's supporters start to ignore or actively disobey orders.

Defections may be public, as when a person openly begins to defy orders, or private, as when a person subtly or anonymously begins to disobey orders or deliberately executes orders slowly or inefficiently.

See also the commentary for the term **loyalty shift** (p. 80).

■ **USAGE IN A SENTENCE**

"Revulsion at the brutality of repression against courageous nonviolent resisters at times has caused individuals serving in the opponents' government, police, or military forces to question both the opponents' cause and the means being used to control the resisters. This may result in unease, dissidence, and even **defection** and disobedience among these members of the opponents' group."[106]

"The skillful civil resistance leader wants to create disruption in order to maximize defections, and optimally wants to employ tactics where relatively small disruptions lead to large numbers of **defections**."[107]

■ **RELATED TERMS**
disobedience, **loyalty shift**, **pillars of support**

42 DEMOCRATIC BACKSLIDING

NOUN
See the term **backsliding, democratic** (p. 29).

43 DEMONSTRATION
(associated with civil resistance)

NOUN

A public action intended to communicate opposition to certain policies or practices and sometimes support for alternative policies and practices. Such action often takes place in a highly visible location and may be conducted by an individual, but ordinarily is conducted by a group.[108]

■ COMMENTARY

Generally, a demonstration refers to a gathering of people who oppose some policy or practice, and/or support some alternative policy or practice. People who participate in demonstrations are sometimes referred to as "demonstrators."

Variations of the term "demonstration" include "mass demonstration," which emphasizes the involvement of large numbers of people, and "protest demonstration," which makes it clear that the demonstrators all oppose a certain policy or practice.

The terms "demonstration," "march" (noun), "rally" (noun), and "protest" (noun) all have similar meanings. However, a "march" always implies movement and walking, while the other terms do not. A "demonstration" is a more general term and generally involves a stationary gathering of people, although in some cases demonstrators could move to another location. A "rally" is a gathering of people, generally stationary, to advocate for or protest against something, often featuring a prominent speaker. A "protest" is a generic term for an action that opposes something, and sometimes the term is used synonymously with the term "demonstration" to mean a public gathering of people.

■ USAGE IN A SENTENCE

"...The locus of the Western Sahara freedom struggle shifted from the military and diplomatic initiatives of an exiled armed movement to a largely unarmed popular resistance from within, as young activists in the occupied territory and even in Sahrawi-populated parts of southern Morocco confronted Moroccan troops in street **demonstrations** and other forms of nonviolent action, despite the risk of shootings, mass arrests, and torture."[109]

"Eager to address the economic crisis and under the influence of US policies, the government [of Argentina] undertook a series of structural adjustments that had a serious negative impact on the middle classes, who revolted in December 2001 with an *outpouring of **demonstrations** known as cacerolazos, the banging of pots and pans outside their homes."*[110]

- **RELATED TERMS**

act of or tactic of commission, assembly, **demonstration**, **dissent** (noun), **freedom of assembly**, **freedom of speech**, **march** (noun), **mass demonstration**, **rally** (noun), **tactic**, **tactic of concentration**

44 DICTATORSHIP

NOUN

A form of government in which total power is held by a dictator or one political entity.

- **COMMENTARY**

A dictator is a person or political entity (junta) exercising absolute power.

In contemporary usage, "dictatorship" refers to an autocratic form of absolute rule by leadership unrestricted by law, constitutions, or other social and political factors within the state. However, some dictatorships do allow elections to be held and have other institutions and practices that appear democratic, but in reality such institutions and practices do not function to restrain the rule of the dictator.

See also the commentary for the term **authoritarian rule** (p. 24).

- **USAGE IN A SENTENCE**

*"More overt forms of nonviolent action occurred in Latin America in the 1970s and 1980s in the face of torture, disappearances and death squads, and led to general strikes and mass protest that helped to end **dictatorships** in Bolivia, Brazil and Uruguay."*[111]

*"The common feature of the cited examples in which **dictatorships** have been disintegrated or weakened has been the courageous mass application of political defiance by the population and its institutions."*[112]

- **RELATED TERMS**

authoritarian rule, despotic rule, totalitarianism, tyranny

45 DILEMMA ACTION

NOUN

An act of civil resistance that creates a set of undesirable choices for a movement's opponent, and therefore forces the opponent to take actions that are damaging and/or costly to itself.

■ **COMMENTARY**

When a movement engages in a dilemma action, it forces its opponent into a predicament. Often the opponent must choose between:

- allowing the act of civil resistance to go forward without using repression (which allows civil resisters to advance their objectives and shows that the opponent is not able or willing to control the situation); or

- using repression against the civil resisters (which could be costly and lead to backfire).

Thus, either option increases the strength of the civil resisters and weakens the opponent.

Dilemma actions often involve a large number of people taking action to defy a very unpopular law or restriction, sometimes in subtle ways that make it very challenging for a movement's opponent to control. For example, when Gandhi led the Salt March in 1930 to violate the British tax on salt, he organized thousands of people to make salt along the Indian coastline using ocean water. It was too costly for the British colonial government to try to police the entire coastline of India to prevent this from happening, but allowing the defiance to go forward would reveal that the British were unwilling to enforce their own laws. They subsequently arrested Gandhi, which backfired and led to heightened mobilization against British rule.

Some dilemma actions involve a small number of people. Such actions often use humor and may be more effective if they involve highly symbolic and well-known participants (i.e., religious leaders, celebrities, and/or well-respected individuals).

■ **USAGE IN A SENTENCE**

*"The first step in designing a **dilemma action** is to review the opponent's policies that place restrictions on the day-to-day activities of the population. The more personal and intrusive the restrictions are, the bigger the dilemma will be for the opponent."*[113]

*"Although not all **dilemma actions** involve a constructive element like bringing humanitarian aid, this is one way to make the dilemma more complicated for the opponent. Similarly, surprises and unpredictability can increase pressure."* [114]

■ **RELATED TERMS**
backfire (noun), **repression**, **tactic**

---

46 DIRECT ACTION

NOUN

An intervention or effort taken by an individual or group to directly change a situation, rather than expecting or asking for other individuals or groups to intervene on their behalf.[115]

■ **COMMENTARY**

In the context of civil resistance, direct action can be disruptive (such as civil disobedience) as well as constructive (such as creating alternative institutions to provide for a community's needs).

In civil resistance literature, the term "direct action" refers to action that is nonviolent. Sometimes you will see this emphasized by adding "nonviolent" to the term, so it reads "nonviolent direct action."

See also the commentary for the terms **nonviolent action** (p. 97) and **civil resistance** (p. 36).

■ **USAGE IN A SENTENCE**

*"**Direct actions** are primarily defined by their confrontative, public, disruptive and possibly illegal nature. They can be done with large or small groups of people. They are most effective when carefully planned, when they focus public attention on injustice in a compelling way, and when other avenues for change have been exhausted."* [116]

*"When 18 people walked onto the construction site of the Seabrook Nuclear Power Plant in New Hampshire on 1 August 1976, it was the first collective nonviolent **direct action** against nuclear power in the USA."* [117]

*"The following day students blockaded the Secretariat, the colonial administrative center for the entire country. It was an audacious action. No group in Burma had ever organized nonviolent **direct action** on this scale. Each gate had rows of students blocking entry and no government employee could go to work,*

effectively shutting down the colonial civil administration. As the police arrived and pried loose students from the gates, other students standing nearby stepped in to fill the breach and the blockade remained in place. The central gates were blocked by women students. At noon, the students felt that they had made their point and ended the blockade by marching around the Secretariat as they collected the students at each gate."[118]

■ **RELATED TERMS**

alternative institution, civil resistance, constructive programme, nonviolent action, tactic

47 DISINTEGRATION
(as a result of civil resistance)

NOUN

A mechanism of change in nonviolent action, in which the capacity of a system or government is so reduced because of massive noncooperation and popular defiance that the system or government falls apart and collapses.[119]

■ **COMMENTARY**

Disintegration is one of the four "mechanisms of change" of civil resistance (the other mechanisms are "conversion," "accommodation," and "nonviolent coercion").[120] They appear frequently in the writings of the scholar Gene Sharp.

■ **USAGE IN A SENTENCE**

*"Once **disintegration** has occurred, it can be very difficult to manage because it is unpredictable what different pillars of support will do when the opponent suddenly falls."*[121]

*"[East Germany] The combined effect of large-scale street protests and massive emigration increased in intensity until the authoritarian system crumbled under the pressure from below. The present interpretation of these events confirms the two main premises of the strategic approach to nonviolent direct action: that the ultimate source of power is not force but popular consent and that the active withdrawal of this consent can lead to the **disintegration** of an authoritarian regime."*[122]

■ **RELATED TERMS**

accommodation, conversion, mechanisms of change, nonviolent coercion

48 DISPERSION, TACTIC OF

NOUN

An act of civil resistance in which participants or resources are dispersed in many different locations, and/or at many different times.

■ **COMMENTARY**

Examples of tactics of dispersion include consumer boycotts and stay-at-home strikes. Because tactics of dispersion like these are spread out over many people and a wide area, they are generally more costly for a government to repress and carry lower risk than tactics of concentration.

■ **USAGE IN A SENTENCE**

*"However, in the face of sustained repression, challengers must be able to shift to **tactics of dispersion**, in which cooperation is withdrawn, such as a strike or boycott. These methods do not provide the state with a tangible target for repression and may overextend the state's repressive capacities due to the lack of a specific target."*[123]

"The wearing of common symbols (as in the Shayfeen.com and Kefaya *campaigns) and the organization of boycotts and stay-aways (most notably in the Iranian Revolution and first Palestinian intifada) are two examples of **dispersed tactics** that enable mass participation while allowing for individual anonymity."*[124]

■ **RELATED TERMS**
decentralized

49 DISRUPT

VERB

To interrupt, disturb, or prevent the normal progress of a process or activity.

■ **COMMENTARY**

See the commentary for the term **disruption** (associated with civil resistance) (p. 57).

■ **USAGE IN A SENTENCE**

"After intense deliberation, first among villagers and later with external actors, San José residents reached the conclusion that

to resist displacement they needed to act collectively, to coordinate and organize themselves to develop a set of behavioral rules of noncooperation that could **disrupt** 'business-as usual' for violent actors."[125]

"**Disrupting** the state's control, resistance movements can drive up the cost of maintaining the system—to the point that its defenders begin to question its future."[126]

■ **RELATED TERMS**
interrupt, intervene, prevent

50 DISRUPTION

NOUN

An interruption, disturbance or problem in a process, event, or activity, which can increase its costs, change its course, or cause the process, event or activity to stop altogether.[127]

■ **COMMENTARY**
A key concept in civil resistance is that nonviolent disruption (i.e., strikes, boycotts, demonstrations, and many other tactics) imposes social, economic, or political costs on oppressive systems. In the face of such actions, it becomes more costly for powerholders to maintain their control. Nonviolent disruption can take many forms—it can be chaotic or peaceful, public or invisible, overt or subtle. For example, a protest or a nonviolent occupation of a building are overt and visible forms of disruption, and they may be conducted in a peaceful manner or in a loud and aggressive manner. A consumer boycott may be a more subtle, peaceful, and less visible form of disruption that can nonetheless be very powerful.

■ **USAGE IN A SENTENCE**
"The South African anti-apartheid movement's ongoing civic **disruption** combined with its call for national reconciliation was able to garner widespread support and create unity for the cause of change, even among some white supporters who had previously supported the apartheid state."[128]

"Any **disruption** of the movement of goods, people, and services can have immediate economic and political costs to the regime."[129]

■ **RELATED TERMS**
disturbance, interruption, **nonviolent intervention**

51 DISSENT

NOUN

The expression of opinions that are different from, and may directly oppose, opinions that are commonly or officially expressed.[130]

■ **COMMENTARY**

Dissent can happen through words, gestures, symbols, actions, or deliberate inaction. It can be personally expressed or collective, strategically planned or spontaneous.

Many tactics of civil resistance express some form of dissent against oppressive acts and policies, and also assert people's rights and human dignity.

■ **USAGE IN A SENTENCE**

"A military coup in 1964 inflicted over two decades of impunity and human rights abuses on the people of Brazil. In 1980, Catholic clergy... began catalyzing civic **dissent** and a unified opposition to the regime. Amid economic deterioration and repression, public calls to end the dictatorship grew, culminating in the broad-based 1983 Diretas Já (direct elections now) movement demanding direct presidential elections."[131]

"The organized expression of citizen **dissent** harnesses a different form of power: civic power. It is expressed through the strategic use of strikes, boycotts, civil disobedience, mass actions, non-cooperation, and over two hundred other nonviolent tactics designed to influence the power establishment and disrupt the oppressor's sources of control and support."[132]

"Iran is home to one of the most innovative and tenacious examples of citizen **dissent** today. In Iran, women are effectively channeling their grievances into a strategic nonviolent campaign to end imposed gender subordination and fight for legal rights. Beyond its own vision of gender equality, the Iranian women's moment is expanding the frontiers of civic action on multiple fronts."[133]

■ **RELATED TERMS**

disagreement, **dissident**, **protest** (noun)

52 DISSIDENT

NOUN

A person who actively opposes or challenges official policy, especially against an authoritarian state.[134]

■ **COMMENTARY**

This term was widely used for individuals and groups who opposed Communist Party regimes in the Soviet Union and other Communist countries, but is now used more widely and is not limited to those circumstances.[135]

■ **USAGE IN A SENTENCE**

"For decades, critics of China's ruling communist party have sought refuge in Thailand. But now it appears even foreign countries aren't safe for political **dissidents** seeking to escape the long arm of the Chinese law."[136]

"From the authoritarian's perspective, internal **dissidents** are easier to deal with—put them in jail, have them disappeared, exiled, or executed. It is not so easy to silence the prestigious Nobel committee, however, let alone the vague collective referred to as 'the international community.'"[137]

■ **RELATED TERMS**
activist, dissenter, objector

53 DYNAMICS
(of civil resistance)

PLURAL NOUN

The processes by which forces are generated, activated, and interact with each other throughout a conflict between a civil resistance movement and its opponent(s) in which the movement is trying to achieve its objectives despite the counter-actions of its opponent(s).

■ **COMMENTARY**

Some key concepts in understanding the dynamics of civil resistance include: obedience/consent as a source of power; the importance of legitimacy in creating obedience (and therefore power); the concept that civil resistance movements can disrupt and impose costs on their opponent through nonviolent tactics; repression by opponents as a means to create obedience in a population; backfire; and defections by the supporters of a movement's opponent. These concepts are all part of the "dynamics" of civil resistance and are central to understanding how various choices by civil resistance movements and their opponents impact the emergence, development, and outcomes of these conflicts.

■ **USAGE IN A SENTENCE**
"We educated ourselves about torture and about the ***dynamics*** *of nonviolence. We watched a film on Mahatma Gandhi. I was more motivated to protest against poverty, but I responded to the discipline of the group. We deliberated and decided to undertake a nonviolent demonstration to denounce torture.*"[138]

"*... if methods of nonviolent action are implemented in a disciplined, organized, and persistent manner, certain* ***dynamics*** *may be activated that contribute to the alternation of power relationships within society. One dynamic that may occur, for example, is that repression, rather than demobilizing a movement, actually contributes to its mobilization.*"[139]

■ **RELATED TERMS**
processes

54 EMPOWER

VERB

To promote the capacity, power, or influence of a group or individual (often through the development of skills, self-confidence, the support of others, and increased self-reliance) to make choices, take responsibility for their own life or their community, exercise their rights, or fight injustice.[140]

■ **COMMENTARY**
Effective civil resistance movements often empower people to take greater control of their own lives and the wellbeing of their communities and societies.

■ **USAGE IN A SENTENCE**
"*The Social Movement against Corruption, launched by Transparency International-Bangladesh,* ***empowers*** *citizens to hold public officials accountable for health, education and local government services through citizen committees and a variety of nonviolent actions, such as information tables outside hospitals.*"[141]

"Mass nonviolent movements, such as those which ousted Mubarak [Egypt], along with scores of other dictators in recent decades, make regime change possible through **empowering** pro-democratic majorities."[142]

■ **RELATED TERMS**
augment, **capacity**, enable, strengthen

55 EMPOWERMENT

NOUN

The process of becoming stronger and more confident, especially in controlling one's life, making choices, and exercising one's rights.[143] **This may happen through positive experiences, the development of skills, the support of others, and building increased self-reliance.**

■ **COMMENTARY**
See also the term **empower** (p. 60).

■ **USAGE IN A SENTENCE**
"... the future of the anti-corruption movement... [involves] incorporating citizen mobilisation and **empowerment**, as well as the inclusion of youth."[144]

"Noncooperation undermines the legitimacy, resources, and power of the state, and the collective withdrawal of cooperation from the state promotes cooperation and **empowerment** among the oppressed."[145]

■ **RELATED TERMS**
agency, **capacity**, **empower**, enablement

56 ESCALATE
(in a conflict)

VERB

To increase the scale or intensity of a conflict.

■ **COMMENTARY**
Escalation often happens deliberately (i.e., by a side choosing to increase the scale or intensity of a conflict) but it can also happen incidentally (i.e., a drought may intensify a conflict). In the

context of civil resistance, escalating a nonviolent conflict can entail increasing pressure on a movement's opponent by choosing more visible tactics, sequencing multiple tactics, or increasing the frequency or magnitude of their implementation.

See also the commentary for the term **escalation** (in a conflict) (p. 62).

■ USAGE IN A SENTENCE

*"Continuing with these methods, the Palestinians added noncooperation to their repertoire in the form of social, economic, and electoral boycotts and resignation from jobs in the British colonial administration. They sustained protests against land grants to Zionists and **escalated** approaches of noncooperation as shops closed across the country."*[146]

*"The major tactic that initiated the movement was [for mothers] to meet in the Plaza de Mayo, in the center of Buenos Aires [Argentina], facing the presidential palace, to protest the disappearance of their children. They wore headscarves with the names and sometimes carried photographs of their children who had disappeared, leaving the military junta baffled about how to respond. They began as individuals searching for their children through legal means in government offices, then **escalated** their tactics by gathering in the Plaza."*[147]

■ RELATED TERMS
increase, intensify

---

57 ESCALATION
(in a conflict)

NOUN

An increase in the scale, geographical scope, and/or intensity of a conflict.[148]

■ COMMENTARY

Escalation may be deliberate by one side of a conflict or unintended. Escalation by one side of a conflict may stimulate counter-actions (counter-escalation) from the other side and further intensify the conflict.[149]

As a result of escalation, a conflict may be extended, for example, to include new areas, population groups, or issues. Or, greater resources or more intense tactics may be used by one or more sides of a conflict.

See also the commentary for the term **escalate** (in a conflict) (p. 61).

■ **USAGE IN A SENTENCE**

"***Escalation*** *of the campaign may be focused on increasing the frequency, intensity, or diversity of grass-roots level activities, such as public events and door-to-door canvassing.*"[150]

"*Almost every nonviolent campaign is an example of conflict **escalation** with peaceful means. These movements can celebrate their victories because they used conflict as a resource to confront injustice, and helped to create a better society in doing so.*"[151]

■ **RELATED TERMS**

escalate, intensification, **tactical sequencing**

58 EXTERNAL ACTOR

NOUN

A group, community, organization, institution, entity, or occasionally a prominent individual, that is not directly engaged at the center of a conflict or struggle, but that takes (or can take) actions that have an impact on the conflict.

■ **COMMENTARY**

External actors may include: states; multilateral institutions (such as the UN, EU, ASEAN, AU); nongovernmental organizations (NGOs); corporations; external funders of various kinds; diaspora communities; media outlets; foreign civil society groups (i.e., church or student groups); transnational civil resistance movements and campaigns; and highly visible, influential, powerful, and wealthy individuals.

In civil resistance literature, "external actors" are often based geographically outside of the country or territory where civil resistance is being waged, although they may have people or offices (i.e., an embassy, a UN mission, an NGO branch office) in a given country or territory. But the emphasis on being centered outside of a particular country gives the term "external actor" a different emphasis than the term "third party," which also refers to groups or actors who are not directly involved in a conflict but may (or may not) be based inside the territory or country where civil resistance is being waged.

■ **USAGE IN A SENTENCE**

"The evolution and use of social audits [an anti-corruption tactic] in Kenya and community monitoring in Afghanistan demonstrate the positive confluence of bottom-up civic initiatives and **external actors**.... In both cases, tactics were adapted at the local level rather than copied from other campaigns and movements in the international arena. The origins of the six-step social audit... in Kenya stem from... [an organization and a] movement in India. Two NGOs... played catalytic roles in disseminating information and lessons learned from this movement [to other communities around the world]."[152]

"**External actors** do not always have a substantial impact on nonviolent movements and successful civil resistance relies on the decisive agency of local people, not foreign forces. But the cases of the United States, Zambia, Mozambique, Poland, West Papua, Algeria, Egypt, and Palestine... show that in some circumstances there are clear benefits to enlisting international sympathy, winning over external allies or, at least, neutralizing traditional supporters of the adversaries. In all of these cases, civil resisters were cognizant of the importance of cultivating international support to further their cause."[153]

■ **RELATED TERMS**

ally (noun), **external support**, **third party**, transnational solidarity

---

59 EXTERNAL SUPPORT

NOUN

Help or assistance that is given by an external actor with the intention of assisting one or more parties in a conflict.

■ **COMMENTARY**

External support could include providing material or economic resources; political or diplomatic assistance; information, training, and skills; humanitarian aid; military aid; or other forms of assistance.

External support can be given directly to a party (for example, direct material support). Or, it can benefit a party indirectly (for example, when an external actor advocates for human rights in a particular country, or advocates for withdrawing support from human rights abusers, without directly naming or supporting a particular human rights movement).

■ **USAGE IN A SENTENCE**

*"The starting point for any discussion of **external support** to nonviolent campaigns and movements must be the local context and the expressed needs of local activists. Decisions about external support should be based on an examination of the place and people in question, cognizant of the fact that no two countries are alike—and therefore no two strategies can be alike."*[154]

*"**External support** can, in some instances, have unintended negative impacts on grassroots mobilization. One such outcome is the 'channeling effect,' which occurs 'when a social movement and its leadership redirect their strategies, goals, and alliances away from the original mission toward those acceptable to funders.'"*[155]

■ **RELATED TERMS**

external actor, external allies, external assistance, external supporters, **third party**, third party support

60 FAILURE

(associated with civil resistance)

NOUN

A decisive lack of achievement of a party's stated objectives in a conflict.

■ **COMMENTARY**

In civil resistance literature, the noun "failure" often refers to the non-achievement of a clearly stated goal (or in some cases multiple goals) by a movement. For example, if a movement's goal is to get a government to create a new policy, the movement can be regarded as a "failure" if it does not achieve this outcome. If the movement only partially achieves its goal (or, if the movement has multiple goals and it achieves only some of those goals), the movement may be called a "partial success." If the movement is able to achieve its stated goals, it is called a "success."

One of the benefits of defining success and failure in this clear way is that it allows social scientists to more easily study and compare movements and their outcomes. This definition of the terms "failure" and "success" is especially common when referring to quantitative research.

However, some authors object to this narrow definition of failure and success, arguing that even if a movement fails to achieve its stated objectives, the movement may succeed at creating other positive effects, and therefore such a movement should still be called a "success" and should not be labeled a "failure."

Thus, one author may call a movement a "failure" because it failed to achieve its stated goals, while another author may label the same movement a "success," because it "succeeded" (verb) or "was successful" (verb + adjective) at achieving certain other positive effects.

See also the commentary for the term **success** (associated with civil resistance) (p. 141).

■ USAGE IN A SENTENCE
*"Despite a few temporary concessions granted by the regime, including multiparty elections in 1990, which were won by the opposition National League for Democracy (NLD), the 1988 campaign [for democracy in Burma] is best characterized as a **failure**, given that Burma remains a highly repressive military dictatorship."* [156]

*"We did not find any structural factors that predetermined the outcomes of... [the campaigns we researched]. For instance, we saw campaigns emerge, mobilize, and succeed even under repressive circumstances, as in the Philippines and Iran, whereas repression is clearly an insufficient explanation for the **failure** of the Burmese and Palestinian campaigns."* [157]

■ RELATED TERMS
goal, **objective** (noun), **success** (antonym)

---

61 FLANK, VIOLENT

NOUN

See the term **violent flank** (p. 153).

---

62 FRAME
(in communication)

VERB

To emphasize and make connections among certain issues, facts, and events "in order to promote a particular interpretation, evaluation, and/or solution." [158]

■ **COMMENTARY**

A communicator (person, organization, government, movement, or the media) frames an issue when they focus attention on certain aspects of an event or issue and draws relationships between these aspects, which impacts how the event or issue is seen or understood by the public. Framing is important for movements because it can determine how the movement's grievances, issues, and the solutions that it advocates will be understood (or misunderstood) by diverse audiences, including its supporters, neutral parties, and its opponent's supporters. For example, police brutality can be framed as an issue of a few bad police doing bad things, an issue of a corrupt system, an issue of bad police training, an issue that illustrates broader national authoritarian rule, and/or an issue of racism and abusing minorities. Framing affects how people interpret a fact or event.

Civil resistance movements often battle with their opponents over who gets to frame key social, economic, and/or political issues (which in turn impacts how people identify root causes and solutions). One side frames the issues, and then the other side responds and reframes the issues.

See also the commentary for the term **frame** (in communication) (noun) (p. 68).

■ **USAGE IN A SENTENCE**

*"Leaders counter self-doubt by enhancing others' sense of self-efficacy, the sense that you can make a difference.... One can inspire this sentiment by **framing** action in terms of what we can do, not what we can't do."* [159]

*"When Papuans exclusively appeal to indigenous identity and Christianity, **frame** their grievances around historical injustices, and communicate their aspirations in ways that emphasize independence [of West Papua from Indonesia], they unwittingly limit their ability to mobilize support from other Indonesians who are overwhelmingly nationalist and Muslim."* [160]

*"There is a perception that working for intermediate objectives means selling out the long-term goal of independence. Yet to build Indonesian support for Papuans and put pressure on the Jakarta government require **framing** campaigns around intermediate objectives like freedom of expression, democracy, environmental protection, corruption, sustainable development, universal access to education and health services, accountable government, and human rights."* [161]

■ **RELATED TERMS**
communication, context, contextualize, **frame** (noun), media, reframe

---

63   FRAME
(in communication)

NOUN

The context within which information is placed, which can impact how an audience perceives and understands that information, and the conclusions they draw from that information.

■ **COMMENTARY**

Communication frames inform how an audience thinks about an issue or event. Selecting frames is important for movements because frames can determine how the movement's grievances, issues, strategy, and the solutions that it advocates will be understood (or misunderstood) by diverse audiences, including its supporters, neutral parties, and its opponent's supporters.

See also the commentary for the term **frame** (in communication) (verb) (p. 66).

■ **USAGE IN A SENTENCE**

"... *a media frame helps form the cognitive structure of our perceptions of reality, and so it can determine what parts of a news story we find most significant. It helps us draw subconscious conclusions about the meaning behind the events in a story. **Frames** can be thought of as metaphors that serve to structure our experience and understanding of the complex world around us.*"[162]

"*In the fall of 2007, by the first week of October, as Burmese students, monks and citizens still hoping for an end to decades of austerity and repression continued to take to the streets in what is now known as the 'Saffron Revolution,' even in the face of violence threatened by the regime, much of the international media had nevertheless appraised the uprising as a failure. News stories began referencing the junta's claim to be 'restoring order' and its promise that life in Burma would soon be 'returned to normalcy.' Life for the Burmese people has not, for many decades, been normal or orderly, but this reality did not seem to faze reporters, most of whom were forced to rely on the regime for information on events transpiring on the streets of Rangoon and elsewhere. Inside the country, activists had a very different story to tell. From their vantage point, it was actually they who were attempting to bring—for the first time in many decades—normalcy and order to Burmese society.*

*The **frames** on the story that emerged in international media, even before public resistance was finally quashed, reinforced several common and hardened beliefs about power, violence and the relationship between the two. These **frames**, which then led to misconceptions about the struggle, may have unintentionally served the interests of the oppressors."* [163]

■ **RELATED TERMS**
communication, **frame** (verb), media

64 FREEDOM
(political)

NOUN

A political condition in which individuals have the power, right, and opportunity to make decisions and take actions that are important to their lives and society and to participate in and make an impact on their society and political system. [164]

■ **COMMENTARY**
Political freedom is related to the idea of rights, because freedom often involves recognized rights to make choices and take certain actions. However, rights to choose and act must be balanced by the fact that such choices and actions should not violate the rights of others.

■ **USAGE IN A SENTENCE**
*"It is common today to place nearly complete reliance on the formal constitution, legislation, and judicial decisions to establish and preserve political **freedom**."* [165]

*"The Chinese leadership had thought that allowing modest religious and social **freedoms** would satisfy the Tibetans enough that they would forgo their more contentious desire for political freedom. But Beijing was wrong. Liberalization—like repression earlier—brought about the opposite effect. The small dose of cultural freedom sensitized the Tibetans to their lack of political freedom, and made them restless for greater change."* [166]

■ **RELATED TERMS**
choice, liberty, **self-determination**

65 FREEDOM OF ASSEMBLY

NOUN
Freedom to gather in one place for a common purpose.

■ COMMENTARY

Article 20 of the Universal Declaration of Human Rights (UDHR) recognizes the freedom of peaceful assembly and the freedom of association. These freedoms are related, and are enshrined in Article 21 (Freedom of Assembly) and Article 22 (Freedom of Association) of the International Covenant on Civil and Political Rights (ICCPR). Freedom of assembly generally refers to less formal gatherings (for example, meetings, public assemblies or protest demonstrations), whereas freedom of association is commonly understood to refer to more formally organized and lasting forms of assembly (for example, trade unions or formal organizations).

These freedoms are often among the first under attack in repressive contexts, and may be restricted under the pretense of national security or protection of sovereignty. Nonviolent activists often promote and safeguard these freedoms by exercising them and resisting efforts to limit or repress them in civic spaces.

See also the commentary for the term **freedom of association** (p. 71).

■ USAGE IN A SENTENCE

"... the **freedom to peaceful assembly** can play an instrumental role in building support for change or reforms, or in voicing discontent." [167]

"Governments often violate the right to **freedom of assembly** as a method of suppressing dissent and critical voices. The right to peaceful protest is indeed a core component to the right to assemble peacefully. However, in many circumstances, peaceful protestors are subject to arrest, violence, threats or intimidation." [168]

■ RELATED TERMS

demonstration, freedom of association, protest (noun)

66 FREEDOM OF ASSOCIATION

NOUN

The right to join with others as part of a group, usually having a common purpose and often exercising the right to assemble and the right to free speech.

■ COMMENTARY

Article 20 of the Universal Declaration of Human Rights (UDHR) recognizes the freedom of peaceful association and the freedom of assembly. These freedoms are related, and are enshrined in Article 22 (Freedom of Association) and Article 21 (Freedom of Assembly) of the International Covenant on Civil and Political Rights (ICCPR). Freedom of assembly generally refers to less formal gatherings, whereas freedom of association is commonly understood to refer to more formally organized and lasting forms of assembly (for example, trade unions or formal organizations). Notably, freedom of association also includes the right to refuse to be part of any such group.

These freedoms are often among the first under attack in repressive contexts, and may be restricted under the pretense of national security or protection of sovereignty. Nonviolent activists often promote and safeguard these freedoms by exercising them and resisting efforts to limit or repress them in civic spaces.

See also the commentary for the term **freedom of assembly** (p. 70).

■ USAGE IN A SENTENCE

"Democracy, rule of law, and **freedom of association** are steps in rectifying the power imbalance that gives rise to the abuse of workers."[169]

"Prior to 1986, actors demanded fundamental freedoms from military dictatorships and governments, including the right to life, **freedom of association**, and freedom from arbitrary arrest. As conditions developed, civilian platforms were adapted, and organizations broadened their objectives, demanding public services, economic and cultural rights, and reform of and participation in the state and public authorities...."[170]

■ RELATED TERMS

freedom of assembly, **freedom** (political), labor union

67 FREEDOM OF SPEECH
(or "freedom of expression")

NOUN

The capacity to hold, express, share, and receive opinions, information, and ideas both within and outside of a society, through a full range of media (i.e., written or spoken words, symbols, music, film, performance, artistic expression).

■ **COMMENTARY**

Freedom of speech is part of a group of interconnected rights (in addition to freedom of opinion, press and information) that collectively fall under "Freedom of Expression." Article 19 of the Universal Declaration of Human Rights (UDHR) states that people shall have "freedom to hold opinions without interference and to seek, receive and impart information and ideas through any media and regardless of frontiers." Freedom of expression was subsequently enshrined in all major international and regional human rights instruments.[171]

In many national contexts, nonviolent movements play a vital role in the safeguard and protection of these freedoms, often resisting efforts to limit or repress them in civic spaces. This is because although freedom of expression is considered a fundamental right, Article 19 of the International Covenant on Civil and Political Rights (ICCPR) allows for restrictions "for the protection of national security, public order, public health, or public morals." Any restrictions must be adopted by law and be 'proportionate.'

■ **USAGE IN A SENTENCE**

"The Polish government was threatened by the emergence of autonomous organizations and by **freedom of speech**, and it responded with an intensification of repression against the unarmed dissidents in order to hold onto power."[172]

"The defamation article in the Indonesian Penal Code is used by officials to clamp down on activists and reformers, and to restrict dissent and **freedom of expression**."[173]

■ **RELATED TERMS**

dissent (noun), freedom of information, freedom of opinion, freedom of press, **freedom** (political), **protest** (noun)

68 GOAL

NOUN

The aim or purpose toward which an effort is directed.

■ COMMENTARY

A civil resistance movement's strategy often involves planning and sequencing actions to achieve short-term goals, medium-term goals and long-term goals. Short-term goals are sometimes called "tactical goals," and long-term goals are sometimes called "strategic goals."

In addition, a significant amount of quantitative research has been done on movements with "maximalist goals," which are defined as goals that result in "fundamentally altering the political order."[174] Maximalist goals include creating a political transition, achieving self-determination or independence, and/or expelling a foreign occupier. In contrast, some movements seek to achieve "reformist goals," which would result in significant policy change within an existing political order.

■ USAGE IN A SENTENCE

*"Most people will struggle and sacrifice only for **goals** that are concrete and realistic enough to be reasonably attainable."*[175]

*"Nonviolent protest—framed in terms of achieving limited **goals**—was widely adopted in the former Soviet bloc from the 1970s, where activists were acutely aware of the danger of Soviet military intervention. The most impressive protests occurred in Poland, where by the 1970s intellectuals and workers made common cause, and major strikes won economic concessions."*[176]

■ RELATED TERMS

objective (noun), **plan** (verb), **strategy**

69 GRAND STRATEGY

NOUN

A comprehensive perspective of how a goal is to be achieved, which includes a concept of what form(s) of action will be taken (nonviolent, violent, institutional or some combination), how resources (human, material, skills and knowledge, time) will be allocated, and how subordinate strategies (sometimes referred to as campaigns) will be applied to achieve intermediate objectives that support the attainment of the ultimate goal.[177]

■ **COMMENTARY**
In the field of civil resistance, a grand strategy states what a civil resistance movement stands for, what it stands against, and the overarching goals that a movement aims to achieve. It also includes major strategic choices, such as the methodology of struggle (institutional means, nonviolent struggle, violent struggle), and how human and material resources will be allocated to that struggle.

The scholar Gene Sharp writes about a four-part framework for analyzing and understanding strategic planning in movements, which involves:

1. Grand strategy (or vision)
2. Strategies (or campaigns)
3. Tactics
4. Methods

These four terms are defined in this glossary, with "grand strategy" serving as the broadest concept of how a movement will evolve. Campaigns relate to the achievement of major intermediate objectives of the struggle, and these intermediate objectives directly support the achievement of the goals of the grand strategy. Each tactic and method relates to the achievement of short-term objectives of the struggle, which directly supports the achievement of goals in each campaign.

■ **USAGE IN A SENTENCE**
"A developed wise **grand strategy** then enables the participants in a struggle to act in ways that cumulatively bring closer the achievement of their objectives in a conflict. This can be done while they simultaneously confront the policies, actions, and repression of their oppressors."[178]

"When planning a strategy, it is most helpful to start planning based on your conception of a **grand strategy**, and then work your way down to the other levels, as opposed to thinking about methods, and then working your way up to a grand strategy."[179]

■ **RELATED TERMS**
campaign (noun), **plan** (noun), **strategy**, **vision**

70 GRASSROOTS

ADJECTIVE

Relating to, originating from, or involving common or ordinary people, in contrast to the leadership or elite of a social organization, political party, or other group or institution.[180]

■ **COMMENTARY**

Civil resistance movements depend on grassroots participation. However, movements may also have some participants who come from more traditional elite backgrounds.

Sometimes people use the term "bottom-up" (as opposed to elite-driven, "top-down") as a synonym for "grassroots." For example, "Civil resistance movements create bottom-up pressure on institutions."

■ **USAGE IN A SENTENCE**

"**Grassroots** anti-corruption initiatives [in Afghanistan] build democracy from the bottom up, not in the abstract, but through practice, [such as] through... citizen-led surveys, and regular reporting activities on the part of volunteer monitors that instilled their accountability in their fellow villagers."[181]

"[The Tibetan Government-in-Exile's] new strategy of 'internationalization,' accompanied by the protests in [the city of] Lhasa, produced two important results that transformed the Tibetan struggle: the support of Western governments and the rise in international **grassroots** activism for Tibet."[182]

■ **RELATED TERMS**

bottom-up, **grassroots** (plural noun), **movement**, **people power**

71 GRASSROOTS

PLURAL NOUN

1. **Common or ordinary people, in contrast to the leadership or elite of a social organization, political party, or other group or institution.**[183]

2. **A general reference to refer to something at the level of a local community.**

■ **COMMENTARY**

See the commentary for the term **grassroots** (adjective) (p. 75).

■ **USAGE IN A SENTENCE**

"The use of violence [by opposition groups opposed to the Pinochet regime in Chile] drove some of the middle class away from participation. A nonviolent resistance continued organizing in the **grassroots**, however, especially the church-based SERPAJ [organization], which cultivated a network of trained activists and developed a strategy for demonstrating against the regime."[184]

"As part of their planning process, effective movements... gather information, listen to people at the **grassroots**, and analyze themselves, their adversaries, and uncommitted third parties constantly through the course of a conflict."[185]

■ **RELATED TERMS**

bottom-up, **grassroots** (adjective), **movement**, **people power**

---

72 GRIEVANCE

NOUN

A social, political, or economic injustice that generates resentment and/or complaints, and may give rise to resistance.

■ **COMMENTARY**

The scholar Gene Sharp sometimes uses the term "grievance group" to describe a group that has grievances.

■ **USAGE IN A SENTENCE**

"A general strike in action is so widespread that the issue for which the strike was called can easily be lost. The responsibility to communicate the **grievance** falls upon those who call for the action."[186]

"Very careful attention to the grievances and issues from the perspective of the **grievance** group is essential in order to determine the stated objective of the coming nonviolent struggle."[187]

■ **RELATED TERMS**

cause, grievance group, hardship, indignity, problem

73 HUMAN RIGHTS DEFENDER
(or "HRD")

NOUN

A human rights defender (HRD) is a person who, alone or with others, acts to promote or protect human rights.[188]

■ **COMMENTARY**

"Human rights defender" originated as a legal/technical term, but one does not need to call oneself a human rights defender or even know the term in order to be a human rights defender, since human rights defenders are identified by what they do (including their actions and the context in which they operate in).

This term has been increasingly used since the "Declaration on Human Rights Defenders" was adopted by the UN General Assembly in 1998.[189] The text of the Declaration formally recognizes the right to defend and protect human rights and is the first of its kind. It provides an operational definition of what a human rights defender is, and reaffirms the rights that are instrumental to the defense of human rights (such as freedom of assembly and freedom of speech). This Declaration and its definition are relevant for civil resisters who seek to "add to their toolkit" and engage with UN institutions and other organizations that operate under this framework, and leverage opportunities specifically put in place for human rights defenders. This may include diplomatic or institutional support, funding, or other types of support.[190]

■ **USAGE IN A SENTENCE**

"[The NGO] Peace Brigades International sees the role of protective accompaniment as 'expanding the space' for local activists and in particular **human rights defenders**."[191]

"Perhaps most importantly, the Declaration [on Human Rights Defenders] is addressed not just to States and to human rights defenders, but to everyone. It tells us that we all have a role to fulfil as **human rights defenders** and emphasizes that there is a global human rights movement that involves us all."[192]

■ **RELATED TERMS**

activist, **dissident**, human rights activist, human rights professional, **organizer**

74 INSURRECTION, UNARMED

NOUN

A popular revolt by a population that had previously submitted to the government or system, but that now repudiates it through nonviolent struggle.

■ COMMENTARY

The term "unarmed insurrection" is sometimes used as a synonym for a civil resistance movement.

■ USAGE IN A SENTENCE

*"The power of **unarmed insurrections**, it seems, comes from challenging the state in an alternative manner rather than through the violent methods of state."*[193]

*"The presence of **unarmed insurrections** can be seen as a sign of healthy, vibrant and pluralistic societies where discontent can be aired. However, the prevalence of government repression as a counter-measure against such unarmed insurrections indicates that the peace in East Asia can be more authoritarian in nature."*[194]

■ RELATED TERMS

campaign (noun), **civil resistance**, **movement**, **nonviolent conflict**, nonviolent resistance, **nonviolent struggle**, uprising

75 LEADERSHIP

NOUN

1. **One or more leaders of an organization, institution, movement, government, or other entity.**
2. **An individual's or group's ability to lead others, which often includes the ability to direct, inspire, motivate, communicate effectively, organize, mobilize, strategize, and execute wise decisions.**

■ COMMENTARY

Because civil resistance movements are driven by voluntary grassroots participation, they are generally not as hierarchical as governments or businesses, and may not have a single "leader" and instead may have multiple leaders in different geographic areas, or among different groups that comprise the movement.

Sometimes civil resistance literature refers to "centralized leadership" (more hierarchical) and "decentralized leadership" (less hierarchical) in movements.

- **USAGE IN A SENTENCE**

*"As soon as the intifada erupted in December 1987, a multi-party central **leadership** (the Unified National Leadership of the Uprising) was put in place to coordinate the resistance, accompanied by decentralised structures on all levels of society."*[195] *(illustrates the first definition)*

*"'Organized resistance' differs from general resistance in that the defenders act in accordance with a call or instructions from an anti-coup defense **leadership** group."*[196] *(illustrates the first definition)*

*"In a situation where the riot police have jumped from their vehicles—crucial here is **leadership**. Someone has to break that fear, stand their ground and create calmness among others. That is leadership."*[197] *(illustrates the second definition)*

- **RELATED TERMS**
authority, legitimacy

---

76 LEGITIMACY

NOUN

The belief that a group's or individual's authority derives from popular approval, or in accord with accepted sources, criteria, and standards.[198]

- **COMMENTARY**

Legitimacy is an important source of power both for established governments and for opposition movements. Sources of legitimacy may include: representing a population's values, morality, culture and policy preferences; a revered origin of a person or institution; tradition; length of career; age; and consistency with society's accepted procedures, constitution, or laws.[199]

"Legitimacy" and "authority" are related terms because they both influence the willingness of people to obey orders. Furthermore, just like authority can be formal or informal (see the commentary for the term **authority**) (p. 25), legitimacy can also have formal and informal aspects.

Legitimacy can mean that a leader achieved their position through a process (such as elections) that is widely accepted as fair in society. This is a formal aspect of legitimacy.

Legitimacy can also mean that a leader is widely listened to and respected and influential, even if they do not have a formal leadership position. This is a more informal aspect of legitimacy. Sometimes this informal element of legitimacy is referred to as "popular legitimacy."

Legitimacy is a critical concept in civil resistance, because movements may not have a formal position of power (formal authority) to command people in society, but if they have popular legitimacy, they can wield great power (informal authority) by spurring widespread voluntary mobilization and civil resistance.

Often, when writers use the term "legitimacy" (or "legitimate"), they do not state clearly whether they are referring to the formal or informal meaning (or both at the same time) of this term. Translators therefore often will have to use their best judgment to decide.

■ USAGE IN A SENTENCE
*"Unity is essential not only for gaining numbers (citizen participation) but for the **legitimacy** of the campaign or the movement's cause and its tactics. In turn, a [movement's] **legitimacy** can help... make [repression] backfire...."* [200]

*"Externally, the loss of **legitimacy** by a regime may make the international community receptive to calls for economic and political sanctions against it."* [201]

■ RELATED TERMS
authority, leadership

---

77 LOYALTY SHIFT

NOUN
A change in support and allegiance by an individual or group, which causes them to discontinue supporting a previous leader or group and become neutral or potentially begin supporting a new leader or group.

■ COMMENTARY
Loyalty shifts may be caused by a change in opinion or sentiment, or by a change in assessment of personal self-interest.

Loyalty shifts and defections are closely related. A loyalty shift is the mental or emotional change that happens within an individual or group, which is not always immediately apparent. A defection is a conscious decision to take action (based on a loyalty shift) to withdraw support from a previously supported leader or group and/or to take actions to support a new leader or group.

See also the commentary for the term **defection** (p. 50).

■ **USAGE IN A SENTENCE**

*"Establishing public awards for whistleblowers and pro-democracy business and labor leaders is another way to incentivize **loyalty shifts** within the pillars propping up Beijing's power in Hong Kong."*[202]

■ **RELATED TERMS**
defection

---

78 MARCH

NOUN

One or more people (often a group of people) walking deliberately in protest or in advocacy in an organized manner, often moving towards a place that is regarded as significant to the issue involved.

■ **COMMENTARY**

The duration of a march may vary from an hour to a day to several weeks, or even longer. Similarly, the distance of a march may be a few kilometers across a particular city or town or over a thousand kilometers across an entire country. During a march, other actions may be taken as well; for example, march participants may carry posters and banners or distribute leaflets to bystanders.[203]

The terms "march" (noun), "demonstration" (noun), "rally" (noun), and "protest" (noun) all have similar meanings. However, a "march" always implies movement and walking, while the other terms do not. A "demonstration" is a more general term and generally involves a stationary gathering of people, although in some cases demonstrators at a demonstration could move to another location. A "rally" is a gathering of people, generally stationary, to advocate for or protest against something, often featuring a prominent speaker. A "protest" is a generic term for an action that opposes something, and sometimes this term is used synonymously with the term "demonstration," to connote a public gathering of people.

■ **USAGE IN A SENTENCE**

"Many people express their discontent by holding **marches** or rallies, often with signs, placards or banners stating their opinions. For instance, the demonstrations held on 15th February 2003—against the invasion of Iraq—were the biggest anti-war demonstrations ever held, with up to 10 million people marching in more than 600 cities around the world."[204]

"Street actions such as protests, rallies, and **marches** are not merely symbolic actions, but strong tactics as well. They can generate social pressure on power-holders."[205]

■ **RELATED TERMS**

act of or tactic of commission, assembly, **demonstration, dissent** (noun), **freedom of assembly, freedom of speech, mass demonstration, rally** (noun), **tactic, tactics of concentration**

---

79 MASS DEMONSTRATION

NOUN

A demonstration characterized by the participation of an extremely large number of people.

■ **COMMENTARY**

See the commentary for the term **demonstration** (p. 51).

■ **USAGE IN A SENTENCE**

"On the second night of the coup [attempt in Moscow in 1991], resistance organizers passed leaflets throughout the city's subway system calling for a mass **demonstration**... the following day."[206]

"[In the Philippines], Lakbayan (people's freedom marches), mass **demonstrations** that became known as 'parliaments in the streets,' and welgang bayan (people's strikes) were only a few of the nonviolent tactics used during this escalatory phase of the struggle."[207]

■ **RELATED TERMS**

act of or tactic of commission, assembly, **demonstration, dissent** (noun), **freedom of assembly, freedom of speech, march** (noun), **mass demonstration, rally** (noun), **tactic, tactics of concentration**

80 MECHANISMS OF CHANGE

PLURAL NOUN

The processes by which change is achieved in successful cases of nonviolent struggle. The four mechanisms are conversion, accommodation, nonviolent coercion, and disintegration.[208]

■ COMMENTARY

The first three "mechanisms of change" in civil resistance were first identified and named by the activist and educator George Lakey.[209] They appear frequently in the writings of the scholar Gene Sharp, who also added a fourth mechanism called "disintegration."

■ USAGE IN A SENTENCE

*"Different campaigns in your movement may rely on different **mechanisms of change** to be successful."*[210]

*"Certain methods are better at achieving certain **mechanisms of change** than others. For example, if your goal is to produce conversion in your target, you may want to use methods of nonviolent protest and persuasion, such as fraternizing, public speeches, vigils, leaflets, or petitions. But if your goal is to coerce your target, you may want to focus your energy more on methods of noncooperation and intervention."*[211]

■ RELATED TERMS

accommodation, conversion, disintegration, nonviolent coercion

81 METHODS OF NONVIOLENT ACTION

PLURAL NOUN

The range and variety of possible acts falling under the definition of "nonviolent action."

■ COMMENTARY

To give a sense of the diversity of methods of nonviolent action, in 1973 the scholar Gene Sharp identified, documented, and classified 198 methods, sorting them into three main categories:

1. Nonviolent protest and persuasion (i.e., demonstrations, marches, rallies)
2. noncooperation (social, economic, and political) (i.e., boycotts, strikes of all kinds)

3. nonviolent intervention (i.e., blockades, nonviolent occupations of building)

Each of these categories of methods has a distinct definition, but in practice methods of nonviolent action may involve aspects of multiple categories. For example, civil disobedience of unjust laws is an act of noncooperation and in some cases it can also be an act of nonviolent intervention and/or an act of protest and persuasion. As another example, a labor strike where workers occupy a factory is both an act of noncooperation and an act of nonviolent intervention.

Notably, the list of nonviolent methods used by movements and campaigns continues to grow as activists continue to innovate and technology creates new domains for nonviolent action. In subsequent years, some have proposed expanding Sharp's three categories of methods, for example by proposing the "establishment of alternative institutions" (involving the creation of a range of alternative social, political, and economic entities) as a fourth general category of nonviolent methods. Some have also used entirely different classifications to categorize nonviolent methods, for example by referring to "tactics of concentration" and "tactics of dispersion" (which are both defined in this glossary).

Within the work of the scholar Gene Sharp, and other authors who draw from his work, "methods of nonviolent action" are also part of a four-part framework for analyzing and understanding strategic planning in movements. This framework includes:

1. Grand strategy (or vision)
2. Strategies (or campaigns)
3. Tactics
4. Methods

The above four terms are defined in this glossary. However, their usage can be confusing because not all writers define them the same way that Sharp does. In Sharp's framework, "grand strategy" serves as the broadest concept of how a movement will evolve. "Campaigns" concern the achievement of major intermediate objectives of the struggle, and these intermediate objectives directly support the movement's grand strategy. Each "tactic" and "method" concerns the achievement of short-term objectives, which directly support various campaign goals of the movement.

For Sharp, "tactics" refers to *how* and *why* a particular "method" is applied. For example, a mass demonstration is a "method," and "tactic" refers to the mass demonstration's purpose and manner in which it is held. Therefore, tactical considerations would involve determining the best day and time on which to hold the mass demonstration, the best location for the mass demonstration, elements of communications and public messaging, and determining which people can best convey the movement's message.

However, many writers do not distinguish these two terms the way Sharp does, and instead use the terms "methods" and "tactics" as synonyms. For example, they may refer to a consumer boycott or a mass demonstration as either a "tactic" or a "method."

■ USAGE IN A SENTENCE
*"The most commonly recognized and employed **methods of nonviolent action** are those of protest and persuasion."* [212]

*"Since... **methods of nonviolent action**, especially those of noncooperation, often directly disturb or disrupt... 'normal' operations, the opponents are likely to respond strongly, usually with repression."* [213]

■ RELATED TERMS
noncooperation, **nonviolent intervention**, protest and persuasion, **tactic**

82 MOBILIZATION

NOUN

The act of organizing a group of people and resources, and/or taking collective action, in pursuit of a particular objective.

■ COMMENTARY
Some people use the term "mass mobilization" to refer to large numbers of people engaged in collective action.

■ USAGE IN A SENTENCE
*"... in 1989, one of the most destructive and repressive totalitarian systems that ever existed, the Soviet Union, imploded largely peacefully from inside. Its relatively quiet demise was brought about not through greater violent power, but as a result of domestic grassroots nonviolent **mobilization** and the resistance of ordinary people."* [214]

*"Mass **mobilization** is important in civil resistance campaigns as high levels of participation make them more resilient and

raise the political costs of repression. However, a contemporaneous violent movement may act as a deterrent for broad-based mass mobilization, because any protest actions are likely to carry higher risk when they occur where there is simultaneous violence." [215]

■ **RELATED TERMS**
collective action, participation

83 MOBILIZE

VERB

To organize a group of people and resources, and/or to take collective action, in pursuit of a particular objective.

■ **USAGE IN A SENTENCE**
*"2013 began with [Colombian] coal miners in Guajira striking for better wages and improved working conditions, followed by miners throughout the country who **mobilized** to show their guild's importance later in July."* [216]

*"A credible revolutionary strategy has three parts: alternative institutions that create examples of the kind of society we want to live in; social movements that **mobilize** popular resistance by opposing the corrupt institutions currently in power; and independent political organizations that enshrine progressive victories in law."* [217]

■ **RELATED TERMS**
deploy, organize

84 MOVEMENT

NOUN

Ongoing, collective efforts aimed at bringing about consequential change in a social, economic, and/or political system. Movements are civilian-based and involve widespread popular voluntary participation. They alert, educate, serve, and mobilize people in order to create change.[218]

■ **COMMENTARY**
A movement (sometimes also referred to as a "social movement") can have varying levels of structure and organization (some movements may be more centralized around a few key leaders

or groups, and others may be more decentralized). A movement may also include formal organizations within it, but a movement is generally larger than just one or more formal organizations, because movements mobilize people who are also outside of formal organizations. Overall, a movement's members agree to at least some common goals and share at least some common vision (of what they stand for, or stand against, or both), which enables collective action to advance those goals.

- Some key aspects of social movements are that they: involve popular, voluntary activity by people in a society;
- involve grassroots participation—they are a bottom-up (as opposed to top-down) phenomenon;
- persist over a period of time;
- seek to make some form of change (which could be to oppose/prevent something, to enact/create something, or a combination of both); and
- often involve distinct campaigns that each contribute to achieving the movement's objectives.

Notwithstanding this last point, sometimes the term "campaign" is also used as a synonym for the term "movement." See the commentary for the term **campaign** (noun) (p. 34), for more information.

■ **USAGE IN A SENTENCE**

"***Movements*** *that win generally mix... their tactics in [a] sequence meant to maximize participation and disruption while minimizing exposure to repression and the collateral damage to ordinary folks.*" [219]

"*Three attributes can make the difference between success and failure for nonviolent **movements** around the world: unity, planning, and nonviolent discipline.*" [220]

■ **RELATED TERMS**

bottom up, **campaign** (noun), civil resistance movement, collective action, **grassroots** (plural noun), **mobilization**, nonviolent movement, organizing, **people power**

85 NONCOOPERATION

NOUN

Deliberate restriction, discontinuance, or withholding of expected behavior or cooperation with a disapproved person, activity, institution, or government.

■ COMMENTARY

The scholar Gene Sharp organized methods of nonviolent action into three categories: "nonviolent protest and persuasion," "noncooperation," and "nonviolent intervention."

The methods of noncooperation are in turn subcategorized into "social noncooperation" (such as ostracism of certain people or groups, or refusal to obey social norms), "economic noncooperation" (such as economic boycotts or labor strikes), and "political noncooperation" (such as election boycotts).

See also the commentary for the term **methods of nonviolent action** (p. 83).

■ USAGE IN A SENTENCE

"**Noncooperation** comprises the most powerful class of nonviolent methods, because most such actions collide directly with an opponent's sources of power."[221]

"... **noncooperation** [by American colonists against British rule] was not limited to a refusal to buy British goods, but extended to all royal laws. Courts were closed, taxes refused, governors openly defied."[222]

■ RELATED TERMS

boycott (noun), **civil resistance**, **nonviolent action**, **strike** (noun)

86 NONGOVERNMENTAL ORGANIZATION
(or "NGO")

NOUN

A private nonprofit organization dedicated to advancing one or more social, political, or economic objectives.[223]

■ COMMENTARY

Many NGOs seek to alleviate human suffering; promote education, health care, economic development, environmental protection, human rights, and conflict resolution; and encourage the establishment of democratic institutions and civil society.[224] Such organizations may be part of a civil resistance movement, but they are not the same as a civil resistance movement, because a movement involves widespread *voluntary* participation of people in society. However, sometimes the efforts of a particular nongovernmental organization can be an important factor in starting a movement or sustaining a movement.

In addition, it is worth noting that some NGOs may oppose a civil resistance movement, or may try to organize their own counter movements. Some NGOs are funded by governments, corporations, and other powerful funders and primarily seek to further these funders' interests.

Some people use the term "international nongovernmental organization (INGO)" to refer to organizations that do work across national boundaries, in contrast to NGOs, which they define as local organizations. However, this is generally a matter of a writer's preference, and many people still use the term NGO to refer to international organizations.

■ **USAGE IN A SENTENCE**

*"**Nongovernmental organizations**, practitioners from past campaigns, and some international agencies and government entities can assist civilian movements in framing and carrying out well-conceived strategies for nonviolent conflict."*[225]

*"An important value of **NGOs** in a nonviolent conflict is that they provide services to the public and thus demonstrate that people need not be totally dependent upon government. NGO activities can weaken the coercive, but subtle, bond that authoritarian regimes require for public obedience."*[226]

■ **RELATED TERMS**
civil society, international nongovernmental organization (INGO), **non-state actor**

---

87 NON-STATE ACTOR
(or "nonstate actor")

NOUN
A large category of groups that are not officially part of any government or multilateral institution. Non-state actors include movements, nongovernmental organizations (NGOs), private corporations, non-state media, terrorist groups, warlords, insurgents, criminal organizations, religious groups,

independent trade unions, independent universities, and diaspora communities.[227]

■ COMMENTARY

The term "non-state actor" has come into more frequent use, particularly to refer to violent groups outside of state control. Increasingly civil resistance movements find themselves having to confront oppression by non-state actors.

However, not all non-state actors are violent, and some (such as certain nongovernmental organizations, trade unions, universities, or diaspora communities) can be beneficial to movements.

■ USAGE IN A SENTENCE

*"One of the most potent anti-corruption strategies the international community can employ is the disruption of external corruption drivers. Such measures can be taken in both national and multilateral settings and involve state and **nonstate actors**."*[228]

*"Mobilized citizens, often together with **non-state** entities and actors, comprise a social force that can exert pressure on the government and other sectors in society."*[229]

■ RELATED TERMS

civil society, international nongovernmental organization (INGO), **nongovernmental organization (NGO)**

88 NONVIOLENCE

NOUN

1. **The practice of abstaining from violence for religious or ethical reasons. In some belief systems, only physical violence is disallowed. In other belief systems, hostile thoughts and words may also be forbidden. Others go even further and prescribe positive attitudes and behavior toward opponents, or even reject the concept of opponents.**

2. **The practice of abstaining from violence (including any or all aspects of violence from the first definition) based on a religious or ethical belief system that also compels adherents to engage in nonviolent action in the face of injustice.**

3. **The use of nonviolent means to bring about social, political, or economic change.**

■ **COMMENTARY**

The first definition of "nonviolence" involves a religious, philosophical, or ethical prohibition against violence.

The second definition involves a religious, philosophical, or ethical prohibition against violence and the added responsibility to engage in nonviolent action against oppression.

Under these first two definitions, the term "nonviolence" is distinct from the definition of "nonviolent action" (or "civil resistance," "nonviolent struggle," and related terms) because "nonviolent action" focuses exclusively on actions and a methodology of struggle, rather than a religious or ethical belief system.

However, the third definition of "nonviolence" has a similar meaning to the term "nonviolent action," because it describes a mode of action, rather than a belief system.

Some famous leaders of nonviolent movements, such as Mohandas Gandhi and Martin Luther King, Jr., preached about nonviolence and nonviolent action together. This has led to the second definition of "nonviolence," which emphasizes a philosophy that prohibits violence but includes nonviolent methods of struggle. Some people refer to such philosophies by adding the name of the relevant teacher, for example, "Gandhian nonviolence" or "Kingian nonviolence." This fusion of nonviolent action with personal ethics is part of what has led to the confusion and mistaken belief that in order to practice nonviolent action, one must adopt a certain set of ethics or become a pacifist. Unfortunately, this terminological confusion in some cases may cause people to misunderstand the nature of civil resistance and to dismiss it.

Other writers recognize the distinction between ethical "nonviolence" and "nonviolent action," but they express this difference by referring to religious or ethical nonviolence as "principled nonviolence," and referring to the practice of nonviolent action as "pragmatic nonviolence" or "strategic nonviolence." This use of the same root term ("nonviolence") to describe different phenomena still can lead to confusion.

In 1973, Gene Sharp addressed this issue directly. In his book *The Politics of Nonviolent Action*, he set out to systematically study and understand the dynamics of civil resistance, and defined his terms to focus only on a methodology of struggle. Since the publication of this book, the field of civil resistance has evolved as a social science whereby "nonviolent action" and religious or ethical "nonviolence" are often regarded as distinct concepts.

Sharp and others have noted that many people who engage in civil resistance do so because of pragmatic and practical considerations, as opposed to personal ethical beliefs. Still, some people use the term "nonviolence" as a synonym for "nonviolent action."

Having three definitions makes the term confusing when used, which is why many writers in the field of civil resistance do not use the term "nonviolence." Translators should use their best judgment about what exactly the term means in the context in which it is used. In some cases, the term "pacifism" may be the best synonym, and in other cases, the term "nonviolent action" may be the best synonym. It is very important to try to capture the writer's meaning accurately with this term, because for example using the term "pacifism" where the intended meaning is "nonviolent action" can lead to a very poor translation.

See also the commentary for the terms **nonviolence, pragmatic** (p. 93), and **nonviolence, principled** (p. 94).

■ USAGE IN A SENTENCE

"Adherents to principled **nonviolence** refuse to use violence because they consider it to be ethically wrong, even when used for a good cause."[230] *(illustrates the first definition)*

"Gandhi emphasizes that **nonviolence** is not just a method of political struggle but also, critically, a matter of spiritual practice and discovery of the truth."[231] *(illustrates the second definition)*

"The style of nonviolent resistance varies a lot according to context. Since the term 'people power' was coined when the Marcos regime in the Philippines was toppled in 1986, and especially since the downfall of Milosevic in Serbia in 2000, some observers have talked about an 'action template' for popular nonviolent action overthrowing a corrupt and authoritarian regime trying to win 'elections' by force and fraud. There are of course similarities between the downfall of Milosevic and 'people power' actions elsewhere. Indeed some of the Serbs who used **nonviolence** creatively against Milosevic have helped to advise and train groups in similar circumstances. However, circumstances vary and each movement has to analyse what will work for them."[232] *(illustrates the third definition)*

■ RELATED TERMS

active nonviolence, ahimsa, **nonviolent discipline**, **pragmatic nonviolence**, **principled nonviolence**, satyagraha

89 NONVIOLENCE, PRAGMATIC

NOUN

The practice of nonviolent action that is guided by practical concerns, rather than strictly ethical concerns.

■ COMMENTARY

The field of civil resistance takes a social science approach to examining why and how nonviolent action and nonviolent movements work, and the dynamics and impacts of this form of conflict. Thus, civil resistance literature emphasizes the practical impacts of engaging in nonviolent action.

In contrast, the term "nonviolence" often refers at least somewhat to ethical or religious beliefs. For more information, see the definition and commentary for the terms **nonviolence** (p. 90) and **nonviolence, principled** (p. 94).

An ethical or religious commitment to nonviolence is not required to effectively wage nonviolent struggle. Many people are drawn to civil resistance because of its pragmatic benefits, and emphasizing these benefits may enable broader participation and coalition building among diverse groups. Terms such as "nonviolent action," "nonviolent struggle," "civil resistance," and "political defiance" are often used to emphasize the practical aspects of this method of struggle and to clearly separate this method of struggle from a particular religious or ethical belief.

However, some writers prefer to use the term "nonviolence" instead of terms such as "nonviolent action," "nonviolent struggle," "civil resistance," and "political defiance." This preference for the term "nonviolence" has led some writers to develop two categories of nonviolence: "principled nonviolence" (which refers to action or views that are ethically driven) and "pragmatic nonviolence" (which refers to nonviolent action that is driven by practical considerations).

These terms may cause confusion in translation because the creation of the term "principled nonviolence" to contrast with the term "pragmatic nonviolence" creates the inaccurate impression that only ethical nonviolence is based on principles and that "pragmatic" nonviolence is not based on principles.

A commitment to ethical nonviolence is not required to effectively wage nonviolent struggle. At the same time, a commitment to ethical nonviolence does not necessarily exclude a pragmatic approach. We think the clearest way to write about this is to have distinct terminology to distinguish between "nonviolence" as an ethical practice and "nonviolent action" as a means of struggle.

Based on the above commentary, translators must decide how best to address the term "pragmatic nonviolence" in their work. Generally speaking, a synonym would be the term "nonviolent action," and hopefully the translation process can help reduce some of the confusion with English language terminology.

■ USAGE IN A SENTENCE

*"**Pragmatic nonviolence** is best understood as the decision to use nonviolence based upon practical strategic considerations. It does not rely on a fundamental commitment to nonviolence which extends to all situations; it may be limited only to the situation at hand. **Pragmatic nonviolence** is based upon the use of proactive, positive nonviolent strategies and actions. It seeks to change the status quo, ranging in individual cases from specific policies which affect a specific group to the overall dynamics of power in a society. With **pragmatic nonviolence**, a people or a movement can choose not to use violence even if there is no traditional or religious basis for that choice in their culture."*[233]

■ RELATED TERMS

civil resistance, nonviolence, nonviolent action, nonviolent struggle, political defiance

---

90 NONVIOLENCE, PRINCIPLED

NOUN

1. The practice of abstaining from violence for religious or ethical reasons. In some belief systems, only physical violence is disallowed. In other belief systems, hostile thoughts and words may also be forbidden. Others go even further and prescribe positive attitudes and behavior toward opponents, or even reject the concept of opponents.

2. The practice of abstaining from violence (including any or all aspects of violence from the first definition) based on a religious or ethical belief system that also compels adherents to engage in nonviolent action in the face of injustice.

■ COMMENTARY

The term "principled nonviolence" is often used to contrast with the term "pragmatic nonviolence."

See also the commentary for the terms **nonviolence** (p. 90) and **nonviolence, pragmatic** (p. 93).

■ **USAGE IN A SENTENCE**

*"Strategic nonviolent resistance can be distinguished from **principled nonviolence**, which is grounded in religious and ethically based injunctions against violence. Although many people who are committed to principled nonviolence have engaged in nonviolent resistance (e.g., Gandhi and Martin Luther King Jr.), the vast majority of participants in nonviolent struggles have not been devoted to principled nonviolence."* [234]

*"Despite the important role adherents of some type of **principled nonviolence** often play, most instances of mass nonviolent struggles are not initiated by them. 'The major advances in nonviolence have not come from people who have approached nonviolence as an end in itself, but from persons who were passionately striving to free themselves from social injustice' (Dave Dellinger, 'The Future of Nonviolence')."* [235]

■ **RELATED TERMS**

civil resistance, nonviolence, nonviolent action, nonviolent discipline, nonviolent struggle, political defiance

---

91 NONVIOLENT
(or "non-violent")

ADJECTIVE

1. An absence of the use or threat of physical violence.
2. Existing or functioning without the use or threat of any form of harm, including causing physical injury, death, psychological harm, maldevelopment, or deprivation.

■ **COMMENTARY**

The most common definition of the term "nonviolent" in the field of civil resistance is the first definition.

Nearly always, when referring to a mode of struggle (i.e., "nonviolent action," "nonviolent conflict," "nonviolent resistance" or "nonviolent struggle"), writers use this term without a hyphen, but some will use a hyphen ("non-violent"). The use of the hyphen is not preferred in English (although it is grammatically correct), as saying something is "non-violent" simply means the absence of violence, whereas often the term is intended to also indicate the presence of a form of struggle as well. Writing the term without a hyphen is an attempt to move beyond a negative connotation (simply the absence of violence) and towards a positive and constructive connotation (the presence of struggle without violence).

The limits of what constitutes "nonviolent" will vary among different movements. For example, while all agree that being nonviolent requires an abstention from the use or threat of physical violence, some may also decide that being nonviolent includes abstaining from any property damage or destruction. In contrast, some nonviolent movements may decide that property destruction is permissible (i.e., destroying machines and vehicles), while still others may think that only certain forms of property destruction are permissible (for example, only destroying one's own property, or only destroying symbols of oppression rather than actual buildings and vehicles).

There is also sometimes disagreement about whether being "nonviolent" prohibits acts that are harmful to oneself—for example, some argue that a hunger strike is violent if the hunger striker dies, or that self-immolation is violent. Others say that these are nonviolent acts because they are not using or threatening to use physical violence on others.

See also the commentary for the term **violence** (p. 152).

The second definition of the term "nonviolent" is often used outside of the field of civil resistance, but still may be used in some cases in civil resistance literature. For example, some people may refer to the need for "nonviolent communication," which is communication that does not threaten another person physically or psychologically. Or people may refer to groups that espouse ethical nonviolence and adopt the second definition of the term "nonviolent."

■ **USAGE IN A SENTENCE**

*"In 1906 Gandhi joined a large group of Indians to protest a new law requiring all 'Asiatics' to have registration cards. After taking an oath not to cooperate with the new regulations, Indians picketed registration offices and burned their registration cards. Over the next several years, thousands of **nonviolent** protesters went to jail, including Gandhi himself—three times. By 1914 their protests and refusal to cooperate with the authorities had mounted to such a pitch that the government withdrew the registration act."* [236] *(illustrates the first definition)*

"If we admit that, in addition to physical and psychological violence, there might also be structural violence, this raises two questions. First, are all these forms of violence to be avoided by

nonviolent action? Second, is there something in common with these different forms of violence that can bring them under a single umbrella, and in particular an umbrella that would allow us to label them all as violent? The first question is easy to answer. **Nonviolent** *action must avoid all three forms of violence."* [237] *(illustrates the second definition)*

■ RELATED TERMS

methods of nonviolent action, **nonviolence**, **nonviolent action**, **nonviolent coercion**, **nonviolent conflict**, **nonviolent discipline**, **nonviolent intervention**, nonviolent movement, nonviolent resistance, **nonviolent struggle**

92 NONVIOLENT ACTION

NOUN

A technique of waging struggle for political, economic, or social objectives without the use or threat of physical violence. This technique consists of:

a. **acts of commission, whereby people do things that they are not supposed to do, not expected to do, or are forbidden by law (such as protests, symbolic actions, nonviolent blockades, and occupations);**

b. **acts of omission, whereby people refuse to do things that they are supposed to do, are expected to do, or are required by law to do (such as strikes, boycotts, civil disobedience, and other forms of noncooperation); or**

c. **a combination of both acts of commission and acts of omission.**[238]

■ COMMENTARY

Nonviolent action, by definition, refers to actions that are *outside* of formal or institutional means of making change. This means that nonviolent action generally does not include voting in elections or following official procedures for complaint (like filing a lawsuit), both of which are processes established by (state) institutions themselves. However, in practice, many nonviolent movements also engage in institutional means of making change, with the view that both approaches can work together and reinforce each other. In some cases, nonviolent action can be necessary to get official institutional methods of change to work effectively.

It is also notable that although nonviolent action takes place outside of institutional channels of making change, nonviolent action can be organized within institutions themselves. For example, state bureaucrats may engage in a strike or slow down.

Nonviolent action can generally be used as a synonym for the terms "nonviolent struggle," "nonviolent conflict," "civil resistance," "nonviolent resistance," "people power," and "political defiance." The common idea behind these terms is the aim to shift power in society through mass withdrawal of consent and obedience by a population. Nonviolent action succeeds by unifying and mobilizing people, sequencing nonviolent tactics to achieve strategic goals, imposing costs on powerholders, and undermining powerholders' sources of power.

When people participate in nonviolent action in a collective and organized way, they are considered to be part of a "nonviolent movement," "nonviolent campaign," or "nonviolent struggle."

See also the commentary for the term **nonviolence** (p. 90), to ensure that the terms "nonviolent action" and "nonviolence" are not confused.

See also the definition and commentary for the term **violence** (p. 152), to better understand actions that are prohibited under the term "nonviolent action."

■ **USAGE IN A SENTENCE**

*"In 1912 in Lawrence, Massachusetts, immigrant textile workers held a 23,000 person-strong strike to work for better wages and more dignified working conditions. This expression of **nonviolent action** became known as the 'bread and roses' strike, for they carried signs reading, 'We want bread and roses too!' The symbolism of the juxtaposition of bread and roses came to represent fair wages and dignified conditions."* [239]

*"Contrary to regular and institutionalized political activity, there is always an element of risk involved for those implementing nonviolent action since it presents a direct challenge to authorities. Thus, nonviolent action is context-specific. Displaying anti-regime posters in democracies would be considered a low risk and regular form of political action, whereas the same activity in non-democracies would be considered irregular and would involve a substantial amount of risk. It would therefore be considered a method of **nonviolent action** in a non-democratic context."* [240]

*"The Indian struggle for national liberation succeeded, not because of the humanitarian views of the British, but because the force of **nonviolent action** undermined the power of British rule, showed that Great Britain's rule in India was based on force*

rather than legitimacy, reduced the justification for violent repression, influenced reference publics in Great Britain, and illuminated the futility of trying to violently repress a nationwide movement of nonviolent action with military force." [241]

■ **RELATED TERMS**

civil resistance, **nonviolent conflict**, nonviolent resistance, **nonviolent struggle, people power, political defiance**

93 NONVIOLENT COERCION

NOUN

A mechanism of change in nonviolent action in which a powerholder is forced to accept the demands of a civil resistance campaign or movement because effective control of the situation has been taken away from the powerholder by widespread noncooperation and defiance. [242]

■ **COMMENTARY**

In nonviolent coercion, a ruler may give orders, but those orders are no longer obeyed by subordinates. Therefore the ruler has no power, and is effectively coerced to accede to the demands of a nonviolent movement.

Nonviolent coercion is one of the three "mechanisms of change" of civil resistance (the other mechanisms are "accommodation" and "conversion") that were originated by the activist and educator George Lakey.[243] They appear frequently in the writings of the scholar Gene Sharp, who also added a fourth mechanism of change called "disintegration."

■ **USAGE IN A SENTENCE**

"In some cases the number of agents of repression—police and troops—may be curtailed as the number of volunteers declines and potential conscripts refuse duty. Police and troops may carry out orders inefficiently or may refuse them completely, potentially leading to **nonviolent coercion** *or disintegration of the opponents as a viable group."* [244]

"Through **nonviolent coercion**, *change is achieved against the government's will as a result of the challengers' successful undermining of the government's power, legitimacy, and ability to control the situation through methods of nonviolent action."* [245]

"When successful, **nonviolent coercion** *is achieved without the consent of the defeated opponent, whose mind has not been*

changed on the issues and wants to continue the struggle, but lacks the capability to choose a viable alternative. The demands are consequently agreed by force rather than by conviction." [246]

■ **RELATED TERMS**

accommodation, coercion, **conversion**, **disintegration**, **mechanisms of change**

94 NONVIOLENT CONFLICT

NOUN

1. **A conflict in which at least one party uses nonviolent action as its means to wage the conflict.**
2. **The application of the technique of nonviolent action in a conflict situation.**

■ **COMMENTARY**

The first definition of the term "nonviolent conflict" is somewhat academic and focuses on the strategic interaction between conflicting parties, when one or more of those parties engage in nonviolent struggle. For example, a person can say that they "study nonviolent conflict" as a way of saying that they study the dynamics of conflicts involving nonviolent movements.

The second definition of "nonviolent conflict" is more of a synonym for the terms "nonviolent action," "nonviolent struggle," "civil resistance," "nonviolent resistance," "people power," and "political defiance." For example, someone can "wage nonviolent conflict" or "wage nonviolent struggle" or "wage civil resistance" and the meanings are the same. The common idea behind these terms is the aim to shift power in society through mass withdrawal of consent and obedience by a population. People waging nonviolent conflict succeed by unifying and mobilizing a population, sequencing nonviolent tactics to achieve strategic goals, imposing costs on powerholders, and undermining powerholders' sources of power.

See also the commentary for the term **nonviolence** (p. 90), to ensure that the terms "nonviolent conflict" and "nonviolence" are not confused.

See also the commentary for the term **violence** (p. 152), to better understand actions that are prohibited under the term "nonviolent conflict."

■ **USAGE IN A SENTENCE**

"The objectives of **nonviolent conflicts** generally include freedom and democracy, respect for human rights, and rule of law as objectives of their struggle; thus the 'means and ends' are not only compatible but mutually reinforcing."[247] *(illustrates the first definition)*

"Because nonviolent revolutions usually bring genuine civil society and democratic government to the countries that they transform, **nonviolent conflict** as a means of 'regime change' can contribute significantly to the effort against terrorism."[248] *(illustrates the second definition)*

■ **RELATED TERMS**

civil resistance, nonviolent action, nonviolent resistance, nonviolent struggle, people power, political defiance

95 NONVIOLENT DIRECT ACTION

NOUN

See the term **direct action** (p. 54).

96 NONVIOLENT DISCIPLINE

NOUN

1. Persistent nonviolent behavior by members of a civil resistance movement, even in the face of provocations or repression.
2. Adherence to the strategy of a nonviolent movement or campaign, including orderly execution of all nonviolent tactics, communications, and codes of conduct, such as remaining nonviolent even in the face of provocations.[249]

■ **COMMENTARY**

The two definitions of nonviolent discipline are similar. Many writers use a narrower definition to refer to the maintenance of nonviolent behavior by activists and organizers, even in the face of repression. Some writers such as Gene Sharp use the term to mean broadly disciplined behavior in accordance with all elements of a strategy (which includes remaining nonviolent).

■ **USAGE IN A SENTENCE**

"... violent repression was not used against the protesters in East Germany despite orders to do so at least in part due to the highly *disciplined maintenance of nonviolence. Given the widespread support for the protesters and their **nonviolent discipline** even in the face of provocation, it is likely that violent repression would have backfired."* [250]

*"People's courts were organized to maintain order and justice within the townships and to promote **nonviolent discipline**, as violence threatened the support that had been cultivated among South Africa's churches, whites, and the international community."* [251]

*"Planners must consider what measures may be taken to keep **nonviolent discipline** and maintain the resistance despite brutalities. Will such measures as pledges, policy statements, discipline leaflets, marshals for demonstrations, and boycotts of pro-violence persons and groups be possible and effective?"* [252]

■ **RELATED TERMS**
discipline, **nonviolent**

97 NONVIOLENT INTERVENTION

NOUN

A large class of methods of nonviolent action which directly interfere with an opponent's activities and operation of their social, political, and/or economic system.

Methods of nonviolent intervention are most often physical (i.e., a sit-in or nonviolent blockade of a road or building) but may be psychological (i.e., hunger strikes or nonviolent harassment of opponents while they perform official duties), social (i.e., establishing new social patterns, communication systems, or alternative social institutions), economic (i.e., establishing alternative economic institutions or nonviolently seizing land or assets), or political (i.e., overloading administrative systems, seeking arrest, or establishing alternative governing institutions). [253]

■ **COMMENTARY**

The scholar Gene Sharp organized methods of nonviolent action into three categories: nonviolent protest and persuasion, noncooperation, and nonviolent intervention. While each of these categories has a distinct definition, in practice methods of nonviolent action may have aspects of one or more categories—for example, civil disobedience of unjust laws is an act of noncooperation and in some cases can also be an act of nonviolent intervention and an act of protest and persuasion. Similarly, a labor strike in which workers occupy a factory is both an act of noncooperation and an act of intervention.

■ USAGE IN A SENTENCE

"Disruptive **nonviolent intervention** may be used in support of methods of protest and persuasion and methods of noncooperation, and creative nonviolent intervention undermines state authority and contributes to the ability of movements to sustain themselves by providing networks that are alternative to state-controlled institutions."[254]

"Certain methods of **nonviolent intervention** can pose a more direct and immediate challenge to the opponents than the methods of protest and noncooperation, and may thereby produce more rapid changes."[255]

■ RELATED TERMS

civil disobedience, civil resistance, disruption, methods of nonviolent action, nonviolent action, nonviolent struggle

---

98 NONVIOLENT STRUGGLE

NOUN

The waging of sustained nonviolent conflict by a civil resistance movement or campaign.

■ COMMENTARY

"Nonviolent struggle" is sometimes used as a synonym for the terms "nonviolent action," "nonviolent conflict," "civil resistance," "nonviolent resistance," "people power," and "political defiance." The common idea behind these terms is the aim to shift power in society through mass withdrawal of consent and obedience by a population. Nonviolent struggle succeeds by unifying and mobilizing people, sequencing nonviolent tactics to achieve strategic goals, imposing costs on powerholders, and undermining powerholders' sources of power.

See also the commentary for the term **nonviolence** (p. 90), to ensure that the terms "nonviolent struggle" and "nonviolence" are not confused.

See also the commentary for the term **violence** (p. 152), to better understand actions that are prohibited under the term "nonviolent struggle."

■ **USAGE IN A SENTENCE**

*"The operation of **nonviolent struggle** is a fluid, changing, interacting process; never static."* [256]

*"What history reveals... is a timeline of many successful **nonviolent struggles**, extending back for more than a century, with protagonists and causes as diverse as humanity itself."* [257]

■ **RELATED TERMS**

civil resistance, **nonviolent action**, **nonviolent conflict**, nonviolent insurrection, nonviolent resistance, **people power**, **political defiance**

---

99 OBEDIENCE

NOUN

Compliance with requests; expectations; commands; laws; or social, political, or economic norms; and/or submission to the authority of another person or institution.[258]

■ **COMMENTARY**

Obedience may arise from free consent, fear of threatened or imposed sanctions, self-interest, habit, a sense of duty, or other reasons.

The words "obedience" (noun) and "obey" (verb) are sometimes used in civil resistance literature as synonyms for the word "consent" (which can be used as a noun or a verb). However, there can be differences in the meanings of these terms in some cases, as outlined in the definitions of and commentary for **consent** (verb and noun) (p. 43 and p. 44) in this glossary.

■ **USAGE IN A SENTENCE**

*"Evidence of defections within the ranks of the military would suggest that the regime no longer commands the cooperation and **obedience** of its most important pillar of support."* [259]

*"The varied methods of noncooperation all involved refusing to do what was ordered or expected, thereby breaking the habits of **obedience** and the bonds of cooperation."* [260]

■ **RELATED TERMS**

acquiescence, compliance, **consent** (noun), cooperation

100 OBEY

VERB

To comply with a request; expectation; command; law; rule; or social, political or economic norm; and/or to submit to the authority of another person or institution.[261]

■ **COMMENTARY**

People may obey for a variety of reasons, including, for example, giving their free consent, or because of fear of threatened or imposed sanctions, self-interest, habit, or a sense of duty.

The words "obedience" (noun) and "obey" (verb) are sometimes used in civil resistance literature as synonyms for the word "consent" (which can be used as a noun or a verb). However, there can be differences in the meanings of these terms in some cases, as outlined in the definitions of and commentary for **consent** (verb and noun) (p. 43 and p. 44) in this glossary.

■ **USAGE IN A SENTENCE**

*"Many [American colonists] came together in crowd actions and mass meetings to protest and served on or supported local resistance committees. They refused to **obey** the statutes and officers of the British Crown, which so recently had been the law of the land. It was these acts of resistance and noncooperation that struck most openly at the Crown's authority."*[262]

*"If people do not **obey**, rulers cannot rule."*[263]

■ **RELATED TERMS**
consent (verb), cooperate, **obedience**

101 OBJECTIVE

NOUN

See the term **goal** (p. 73).

102 OMISSION, ACT OF OR TACTIC OF

NOUN

An act of civil resistance in which people refuse to do things that they are supposed to do, are expected to do, or are required by law to do.[264]

■ **COMMENTARY**

Examples of acts of omission include labor strikes, boycotts of all kinds, refusal to pay taxes or utility bills, withdrawal of deposits and investments, and refusal to commemorate or celebrate public or religious holidays.

In the field of civil resistance, an act of omission is always intentional. This makes its meaning narrower than in general English usage, in which an act of omission could also be unintentional.

The root of the word "omission" is the verb "omit," which means to leave out or exclude something.

■ **USAGE IN A SENTENCE**

*"Some of the most effective nonviolent campaigns in past independence struggles were built on **acts of omission**— US colonies' non-exportation and non-importation of British-made products, and the Indian boycott of British textiles come to mind—and are therefore difficult to capture on film or in photos...."* [265]

■ **RELATED TERMS**

act of commision, **tactic of commission**, **boycott** (noun), **civil disobedience**, **civil resistance**, noncooperation, **nonviolent action**, **nonviolent conflict**, nonviolent resistance, **nonviolent struggle**, **strike** (noun), tax refusal

103 OPPONENT

NOUN

A group, institution, government, or specific individual who competes or fights against others in a contest, game, argument, or struggle for power and control.[266]

■ **USAGE IN A SENTENCE**

*"When nonviolent protagonists maintain discipline, they not only delegitimize the **opponents**' violence, but they also gain credibility, stature, and, ultimately, power."* [267]

*"Unless campaigns find ways to mobilize mass participation, disrupt the normal order of things and deprive **opponents** of their means of maintaining the status quo, even the most righteous causes fall flat."* [268]

■ **RELATED TERMS**

adversary, enemy

104 OPPOSITION GROUP

NOUN

A political party or civil resistance campaign or movement that is actively contesting power from a government, institution, or dominant elite.[269]

■ **USAGE IN A SENTENCE**

"While there have been instances where threats of nonviolent coercion have resulted in victory for **opposition groups**, threats without a credible capacity to act do damage to any movement, as happened in Zimbabwe in 2002 when two calls for a general strike failed to materialize."[270]

"Internally, members of a regime are more likely to shift loyalty towards nonviolent **opposition groups** than toward violent opposition groups."[271]

■ **RELATED TERMS**
campaign (noun), **movement**

105 ORGANIZER

(in the context of civil resistance)

NOUN

A person who is actively involved in developing and implementing a movement or campaign and devising strategy and tactics (as opposed to just participating in a movement's public actions). This individual works to systematically arrange and plan a united effort, and to recruit others to join this effort.

■ **COMMENTARY**

The term "organizer" and the term "activist" are sometimes used as synonyms in civil resistance literature. However, the emphasis of the term "organizer" is on building and planning a movement and the emphasis of the term "activist" is on taking action as part of a movement. The term "organizer" generally indicates a deeper level of involvement in the development of a movement than the term "activist."

At the same time, activists can build and plan movements and organizers usually take action as part of a movement, so the difference in emphasis is not always significant. It depends on the context in which the term is used.

■ **USAGE IN A SENTENCE**

"Civil resistance movement **organizers** face many common challenges, including developing a unifying vision, building trust among different communities, eliciting widespread participation, coordinating coherent local and national strategies, training participants committed to nonviolent action, and withstanding repression."[272]

"The primary **organizer**, Leymah Gbowee, led a delegation of [Liberian] women to Ghana in June 2003 when it was announced that peace talks would be held in Accra. After six weeks of failed talks and continued violence, Gbowee called for more women to come to the hotel where the men were meeting, to participate in a sit-in outside the negotiating room, and to block the doors and windows until a peace agreement was signed."[273]

■ **RELATED TERMS**
activist, dissident

---

106 PARALLEL INSTITUTION

NOUN

A social, cultural, economic or governance structure that a nonviolent movement builds as an alternative to or substitute for existing institutions that are oppressive or insufficient at meeting people's needs. Such structures are independent of official social, cultural, economic, or government institutions.

■ **COMMENTARY**

Parallel institutions can help a movement to function, build and sustain its capacity, support its tactics, increase its self-reliance and legitimacy, and provide for the needs of its supporters. Such institutions may be formal or informal.

Examples include: alternative governments, media, unions, agriculture, professional associations, financial organizations, civic organizations, and religious organizations. Clubs and social organizations may also be examples of parallel institutions.

Some theorists such as Gene Sharp believe parallel institutions should be built at the end of a campaign, but others such as Gandhi claim that building parallel institutions should be a campaign's first step.[274]

The terms "parallel institution" and "alternative institution" are similar. However, "alternative institution" is a more general term that could include any institution that a nonviolent movement builds, whereas a "parallel institution" is an institution that a nonviolent movement builds as a substitute to an existing (and generally formal and official) institution.

- **USAGE IN A SENTENCE**

*"It is necessary that alternative or **parallel institutions** be in existence to accept the transfer of public loyalty [from the government to the democracy movement]."* [275]

*"Sometimes **parallel institutions** can even amount to an alternative state, as in Kosovo during the 1990s. After Milosevic revoked the province's autonomy in 1989, the Albanians created an unofficial presidency, a foreign ministry, health care organizations, and educational institutions."* [276]

- **RELATED TERMS**
alternative institution, **constructive programme**, organization, parallel government

107 PEOPLE POWER

NOUN

1. **The use of civil resistance by large numbers of mobilized people in a society.**
2. **The "capacity of a mobilized population using nonviolent forms of struggle to make political and social change."**[277]

- **COMMENTARY**

The term "people power" was first used in 1986 in the Philippines to describe the outpouring of popular opposition and mass demonstrations against the dictator Ferdinand Marcos.[278]

"People power" has subsequently been frequently used in civil resistance literature as a synonym for the terms "nonviolent struggle" and "civil resistance." It can also be used to refer to the potential power of a mobilized population using civil resistance.

However, the term has also been used outside of the context of nonviolent movements to refer to significant public support for a particular person or cause. For example, political candidates or organizations will sometimes say that their cause is driven by "people power," even though the people they are referring to may not be engaged in civil resistance at all.

■ **USAGE IN A SENTENCE**

"In 2010, twenty-five years after the generals [in Brazil] were pushed away, the Ficha Limpa ['Clean Slate'] movement wielded **people power** once again—this time to root out graft, abuse, and unaccountability in the electoral system, and to restore legitimacy to Brazil's hard-won democracy."[279]

"Regimes are sustained not merely by their material power, including mechanisms of coercion, but also or primarily by the apathy or ignorance of the common people. The dormant **people power** becomes apparent with a sudden or gradual collective withdrawal of consent and mass disobedience. This force, according to Mohandas Gandhi (Mahatma), gains its strength from the fact that 'even the most powerful cannot rule without the co-operation of the ruled.'"[280]

■ **RELATED TERMS**

civil resistance, nonviolent action, nonviolent conflict, nonviolent resistance, **nonviolent struggle, political defiance**

108 PILLARS OF SUPPORT

PLURAL NOUN

The institutions of society that supply a government, corporation, or other system with power to maintain its rule. Each "pillar" is an institution that supports the power structure of a given regime, corporation, or system.[281]

■ **COMMENTARY**

Examples of pillars of support are security services, the judiciary, moral and religious groups that support a particular regime, labor groups, business and investment groups, and any state-controlled media.

"Pillars of support" is a concept that is useful in strategic planning. Organizers might identify all of the pillars of support of their opponent, analyze each of these pillars, and then develop campaigns, tactics, and communications aiming to get people in one or more pillars to shift their behavior and remove their support from the movement's opponent.

The concept of pillars of support is generally applied to analyzing governments, but it can be used to identify the power structure of other entities, such as corporations.

The term "pillars of support" was first introduce by educator and strategist Robert Helvey. Some people use the term "pillars of power" as a synonym.

■ **USAGE IN A SENTENCE**

*"Nonviolent campaigns tend to attract far more participants than their violent counterparts. This allows nonviolent campaigns to create or exploit cracks within the regime's **pillars of support** (economic elites, business elites, security forces, state media and civilian bureaucrats)."* [282]

*"The police refused to maintain roadblocks established to keep civilian protesters from entering Belgrade, and the armed forces refused to intervene on behalf of Milosevic... The withdrawal of these two **pillars of support** was a result of intensive efforts to convince members of the military, police, and government that democratic change would not lessen their importance."* [283]

■ **RELATED TERMS**
institution, organization, **power** (noun)

---

109 PLAN

VERB

The process of deciding how to achieve a goal. Often this process [sometimes referred to as "the planning process"] involves gathering and analyzing a situation, exploring options, and then deciding to allocate resources to a series of steps, actions, and/or activities in order to achieve a desired outcome.

■ **COMMENTARY**

Planning is sometimes referred to as one of the three key attributes of successful nonviolent movements, together with unity and nonviolent discipline.

Planning may be focused on short-term objectives and actions, and/or intermediate and long-term objectives and sequences of actions.

Some authors prefer to use the term "strategic planning" instead of "planning." In civil resistance literature, often the use of the word "planning" implies that strategic thinking will be part of the process. The term "strategic planning" emphasizes that strategic and structured thinking should be part of the planning process.

When referring to planning for short-term goals, some authors use the term "tactical planning."

■ USAGE IN A SENTENCE

"As part of their **planning** process, effective movements formally or informally gather information, listen to people at the grassroots, and analyze themselves, their adversaries, and uncommitted third parties constantly through the course of a conflict."[284]

"It was our experience, three weeks later when the Summit of the Americas was held in Québec City that the lack of strategic **planning** and nonviolent discipline [by the movement] led to ruthless repression."[285]

■ RELATED TERMS
strategic plan, strategy, tactical sequencing

110 PLAN

NOUN

A list or set of steps and actions to be taken in order to achieve a desired outcome.

■ COMMENTARY

A plan may be simple and designed to achieve a single goal, or it may be complex and include several short-term, intermediate, and long-term goals in a sequence.

In civil resistance literature, it is often emphasized that a plan for a particular tactic or campaign should fit into a larger strategy for the movement as a whole.

See also the commentary for the term **strategic plan** (p. 135).

■ USAGE IN A SENTENCE

"A campaign is a **plan** for the conduct of each major phase within a grand strategy. Each campaign has a specific objective (or objectives) that helps to support the overall goals of the grand strategy. Each campaign also has a **plan** for how it shall develop, and how its separate components (such as tactics and methods) can fit together to contribute to its success."[286]

"In either case, whether your opponent is coerced or if its entire system is disintegrated, your movement must have a **plan** ready for how to transfer to a post-conflict state. A collapsed opponent must be replaced by something new, or else it will return. This shows the importance of making advance **plans** (before you have achieved victory) for how your movement will handle the transfer of power after you have achieved victory."[287]

■ **RELATED TERMS**
strategic plan, strategy, tactical sequencing

---

111 POLITICAL DEFIANCE

NOUN

The use of civil resistance against a government's ongoing rule and policies.

■ **COMMENTARY**

"Political defiance" can generally be used as a synonym for the terms "nonviolent action," "nonviolent struggle," "nonviolent conflict," "civil resistance," "nonviolent resistance," and "people power." The common idea behind these terms is the aim to shift power in society through mass withdrawal of consent and obedience by a population. Political defiance succeeds by unifying and mobilizing people, sequencing nonviolent tactics to achieve strategic goals, imposing costs on powerholders, and undermining powerholders' sources of power.

When people participate in political defiance in a collective and organized way, they are often said to be part of a "civil resistance movement," "civil resistance campaign," or "nonviolent struggle."

The term "political defiance" was first used by educator and strategist Robert Helvey, when he found that Burmese dissidents he encountered were more receptive to this term than other terms such as "nonviolent action" or "nonviolent struggle." The term "political defiance" was subsequently popularized in the literature by the scholar Gene Sharp in his famous short booklet *From Dictatorship to Democracy: A Conceptual Framework for Liberation*, which was originally written for Burmese dissidents, and has now been translated into over 20 languages.

■ **USAGE IN A SENTENCE**

"In March 1960 [South Africa], 50,000 people engaged in **political defiance** by descending on police stations without the requisite passes."[288]

"During two weeks in April 1957 [Colombia], a mass **political defiance** was able to topple Rojas' dictatorial regime through the use of various non-violent techniques."[289]

■ **RELATED TERMS**
civil resistance, **nonviolent action**, **nonviolent conflict**, nonviolent resistance, **nonviolent struggle**, **people power**

---

112 POLITICAL JIU-JITSU

NOUN
See the term **backfire** (noun) (p. 27)

■ **COMMENTARY**
The term "political jiu-jitsu" was originally developed by the scholar Gene Sharp.[290] He used it in reference to the Japanese martial art of jiu-jitsu that focuses on the concept that a smaller, weaker person can successfully defend against a bigger, stronger, heavier opponent by using proper technique and leverage, for example, by using the opponent's weight against him.

However, the term "backfire" is more commonly used in the field of civil resistance than the term "political jiu-jitsu."

■ **USAGE IN A SENTENCE**
"By choosing to fight with a technique which makes **political jiu-jitsu** possible, the nonviolent resisters unleash forces which may be more difficult for the opponent to combat than is violence."[291]

"*Political jiu-jitsu* operates in only some cases where major brutalities are inflicted on clearly nonviolent and courageous resisters."[292]

■ **RELATED TERMS**
backfire (noun), **backlash**

---

113 POLITICAL NONCOOPERATION

NOUN
The withdrawal from, or active refusal to engage in, expected or mandated political activity or participation in the political system.[293]

■ **COMMENTARY**
"Political noncooperation" is part of a large class of methods of nonviolent action known broadly as "noncooperation." The methods of noncooperation are classified in the subcategories of social noncooperation (such as ostracism of certain people or

groups, or refusal to obey social norms), economic noncooperation (such as economic boycotts and labor strikes), and political noncooperation (such as boycotting elections, reluctant or slow compliance with government orders, or refusal to assist or provide information to a government).

■ **USAGE IN A SENTENCE**

"**Political noncooperation** requires development of alternative social and political institutions, potentially leading to parallel government." [294]

"A collateral benefit of **political noncooperation** is that it also tends to strengthen civil society." [295]

■ **RELATED TERMS**

disobedience, **methods of nonviolent action, noncooperation**, withdraw consent

---

114 POLITICAL POWER

NOUN

The capacity or ability to determine and implement official policies and practices for a society by directing or influencing the course of events or the behavior of others.[296]

■ **COMMENTARY**

Political power may be wielded by the institutions of government, or in opposition to the government by dissident groups and organizations. Political power may be directly applied in a conflict, or it may be held as a reserve capacity for possible later use.[297]

■ **USAGE IN A SENTENCE**

"In very extreme applications of widespread determined noncooperation, even a highly oppressive regime can simply fall to pieces. This impact of noncooperation can be produced by extensively and persistently restricting or withholding the sources of **political power**." [298]

"All rulers are dependent for their positions and **political power** upon the obedience, submission, and cooperation of their subjects." [299]

■ **RELATED TERMS**

authority, capacity, legitimacy, pillars of support, power, sanctions (plural noun), **skills, sources of power**

115 POLITICAL SPACE

NOUN

The range of opportunities that people have to express safely and freely, through words or actions, their preferences and to influence political processes and outcomes. [300]

■ COMMENTARY

The relative degree of political space may be placed on a continuum from open and inclusive to closed and exclusive. Political space is considered open if citizens are able to communicate their preferences, organize, act individually and collectively, and engage government without restrictions or harassment. Citizens can occupy existing space, take steps to expand it, or create new spaces where rights of assembly, expression and association are freely exercised.[301]

■ USAGE IN A SENTENCE

"... [the] act of collective resistance can... generate **political space**, and the skillful implementation of methods of nonviolent action can erase decades of fear and apathy and empower a populace." [302]

"Despite this lack of **political space** [in Burma], a political opposition calling for an end to authoritarian rule developed after the military suppressed mass demonstrations in 1988." [303]

■ RELATED TERMS
democracy, **freedom** (political), human rights

116 POLITICAL TRANSITION

NOUN

See the term **transition, political** (p. 148).

117 POWER

NOUN

The capacity or ability to have an impact on other individuals, groups, institutions, one's environment, and/or society.

■ **COMMENTARY**

Power may be exerted through political means, economic means, social means, or a combination thereof. Analyzing power and power structures is at the heart of the study and practice of civil resistance.

Some writers and practitioners identify three different kinds of power:

1. "Power-over" refers to the power of dominance in which the will of one person or group prevails.
2. "Power-with" refers to finding common ground among different people and building collective strength.
3. "Power-to" is an enabling power, derived from acquisition of knowledge or a particular skill.[304]

See also the commentary for the term **political power** (p. 115).

■ **USAGE IN A SENTENCE**

*"Nonviolent action... wields **power** by creating shifts in people's loyalties, behavior and obedience patterns at a collective level."*[305]

*"When people suspend cooperation, when they deny their consent to the ruling system, they are using **power** they intrinsically possess and coercing the government to deal with their demands."*[306]

■ **RELATED TERMS**

authority, capacity, legitimacy, pillars of support, political power, sanctions (plural noun), **skills, sources of power**

118 POWERHOLDER

(or "power holder" or "power-holder")

NOUN

A person or institution with power. This can apply to state or non-state actors. The source of the power can be formal or informal.

■ **COMMENTARY**

The term "powerholder" is used in civil resistance literature as a broad term to describe people or institutions that possess power. It often refers to a person or institution that a movement seeks to influence, including a movement's opponent.

For reference, "power" is defined as "the capacity or ability to have an impact on other individuals, groups, institutions, one's environment, and/or society."

See also the commentary for the term **power** (noun) (p. 116).

■ **USAGE IN A SENTENCE**

"Therein lies the strategic advantage of nonviolent resistance to curb corruption: it consists of extrainstitutional methods of action to push for change, when **powerholders** are corrupt or unaccountable and institutional channels are blocked or ineffective."[307]

"People power pressured Indonesia's leader to take specific measures targeting corruption and impunity. It encouraged transparency and won a degree of accountability from government and economic **powerholders**."[308]

"IWA's [Integrity Watch Afghanistan's] strategic assessment identified the various **powerholders** impacting reconstruction: relevant national ministries and agencies, provincial departments, donors, the military, contractors and subcontractors, and the media. Within these pillars they assessed who had decisionmaking authority as well as those who had institutional power that could be tapped. The civic leaders wanted the overall program to gain strong allies and momentum before corruptors understood its impact, attempted to thwart it, or retaliated."[309]

■ **RELATED TERMS**
authority, capacity, legitimacy, pillars of support, political power, power, sanctions (plural noun)**, skills, sources of power**

119 PRAGMATIC NONVIOLENCE

NOUN

See the term **nonviolence, pragmatic** (p. 93).

120 PRINCIPLED NONVIOLENCE

NOUN

See the term **nonviolence, principled** (p. 94).

121 PROTEST

VERB
1. **To express objection or disapproval through words or action.**[310]
2. **To assemble with others to collectively demonstrate disapproval or objection to particular policies, practices, or viewpoints.**

■ **COMMENTARY**

Protesting (expressing disapproval) can be done in many different ways. For example, one could say "People protested the leader's policies by displaying symbols, chanting slogans, boycotting businesses, and engaging in acts of civil disobedience."

The noun "protest" often refers to a demonstration, but the verb form is less assumed to be tied to this particular tactic, although the verb can refer to a demonstration as well (as in the second definition). Such a demonstration could take place in person or virtually (online).

Context will reveal how the meaning of the word should be interpreted in a sentence.

See also the commentary for the term **protest** (noun) (p. 120).

■ **USAGE IN A SENTENCE**

"In 1896, Britain again tried to introduce direct taxation—the house tax. Women in Accra [Ghana] **protested** nonviolently, marching to Government House and noisily refusing to disperse when Governor William Maxwell would not meet them. They next sent a petition to the colonial secretary in London. While this did not change British policy (neither did the 1898 Hut Tax War in Sierra Leone), it succeeded in rallying the support of King Tackie and other Accra kings."[311]

"Women **protested** against the eviction of peasants from farmland purchased by Zionist colonies and agents. In the late 1920s and early 1930s, women organized a silent procession to exhibit their disapproval of the mandate's policies, submitted statements to each diplomatic consulate, and sent protest telegrams to Queen Mary."[312]

■ **RELATED TERMS**

act of or tactic of commission, demonstrate, dissent (verb), **freedom of assembly**, **freedom of speech**, march (verb), rally (verb), **tactics of concentration**

122 PROTEST

NOUN
1. A statement or action expressing objection or disapproval.[313]
2. An assembly of people who are collectively demonstrating disapproval or objection to particular policies, practices, or viewpoints.

■ COMMENTARY

The term "protest" technically refers to the act of expressing disapproval (which can be done in many different ways), but in civil resistance literature it is often used to mean a "march" or "demonstration" (as in the second definition). Such a protest could take place in person or virtually (online). People who participate in these acts are often referred to as "protesters."

Context will reveal how the meaning of the word should be interpreted in a sentence. For example, saying "Many people attended the protest" would imply that "protest" is being used as a synonym for the word "demonstration." On the other hand, the scholar Gene Sharp refers to "methods of protest and persuasion" as one of the three major categories of nonviolent methods, and this category includes tactics such as making speeches, distributing flyers, writing letters, giving mock awards, singing as a form of expression, painting political symbols or slogans, as well as demonstrations and marches.

The terms "protest" (noun), "march" (noun), "demonstration" (noun), and "rally" (noun), all have similar meanings. A "protest" is a generic term for an action that opposes something, and sometimes the term is used synonymously with the term "demonstration" or "march," to mean a public gathering of people. A "march" always implies movement and walking. A "demonstration" is a more general term and typically involves a stationary gathering of people, although in some cases demonstrators at a demonstration could move to another location. A "rally" is a gathering of people, generally stationary, to advocate for or protest against something, often featuring a prominent speaker.

■ USAGE IN A SENTENCE

"In 1989, **protests** and strikes that became known as the Velvet Revolution led to a peaceful transition from communism in Czechoslovakia."[314]

"[Nonviolent methods of] **protest** *and persuasion help overcome apathy, acquiescence, and fear; promote solidarity; and signal to third parties the existence of an unjust and intolerable situation."* [315]

■ RELATED TERMS
act of or tactic of commission, assembly, **demonstration**, **dissent** (noun), **freedom of assembly**, **freedom of speech**, **march** (noun), **mass demonstration**, **rally** (noun), **tactic**, **tactics of concentration**

123 RALLY

NOUN

A mass gathering of people engaging in political protest or showing support for a cause, group, or leader. [316]

■ COMMENTARY
A rally often has a particular goal and speakers who make speeches to the people who are assembled.

The terms "rally" (noun), "march" (noun), "demonstration" (noun), and "protest" (noun) all have similar meanings. A "rally" is a gathering of people, generally stationary, to advocate for or protest against something, often featuring a prominent speaker. A "march" always implies movement and walking, while the other terms do not. A "demonstration" is a more general term and typically involves a stationary gathering of people, although in some cases demonstrators at a demonstration could move to another location. A "protest" is a generic term for an action that opposes something, and sometimes the term is used synonymously with the term "demonstration," to mean a public gathering of people.

■ USAGE IN A SENTENCE
"On February 21, students [in East Pakistan] from local schools and colleges formed processions that joined a mass **rally** *at the Aswinikumar town hall. A mile-long demonstration moved from the town hall along the main roads of the town."* [317]

"The next day, workers gathered for a **rally** *on the outskirts of Delano [California]. David Havens, a local clergyman, stood before the crowd and started a dramatic reading of Jack London's definition of a strikebreaker... Havens was immediately arrested while the cameras were rolling, and suddenly the strikers had a protest issue that would resonate throughout the state."* [318]

■ **RELATED TERMS**
act of or tactic of commission, assembly, **demonstration**, **dissent** (noun), **freedom of assembly**, **freedom of speech**, **march** (noun), **mass demonstration**, **rally** (noun), **tactic**, **tactics of concentration**

124 REPRESS
(in the context of civil resistance)

VERB
To use pressure or force against an individual or group in order to control or subdue the individual or group or their activity.

■ **COMMENTARY**
See the commentary for the term **repression** (p. 122).

■ **USAGE IN A SENTENCE**
"Regimes often seek to **repress** any form of political dissent. Yet in many cases the intensity and regularity of this repression varies depending on whether the dissent is violent or nonviolent. For instance, the regime may choose to repress violent resistance more strongly than nonviolent resistance because it perceives violence as more directly threatening its power, or because the repression of violent resistance will not lead to external condemnation."[319]

"Chenoweth and Stephan argue that security forces are less likely to **repress** protesters when they have personal connections to the campaign. For example, police facing protesters in Serbia's 'Bulldozer Revolution' of 2000 reported that they refused to follow orders to fire on the protesters because they knew their children were among them."[320]

■ **RELATED TERMS**
punish, **repression**, **violence**

125 REPRESSION
(in the context of civil resistance)

NOUN
The use of pressure or force against an individual or group in order to control or subdue the individual or group.

■ **COMMENTARY**

Repression may involve the use of violence, administrative means (such as arrests and trials, or monetary fines), or other forms of pressure (such as firing from a job). In civil resistance literature, the term is often used to describe violent measures or arrests that a government [or other entity] orders to either prevent the development or the expression of opposition, or to punish, crush, or destroy existing opposition.

These measures may include police activities, surveillance, arrests, trials, imprisonment, crowd control measures, beatings, shootings, terror, concentration camps, intimidation, torture, economic privations (i.e., fines or job dismissal), or other forms of pressure. Some forms of repression are more directly violent (i.e., beatings and shootings), while others are more administrative (i.e., arrests, fines, and trials).[321]

■ **USAGE IN A SENTENCE**

*"Violent incidents by members of a movement can dramatically reduce its legitimacy while giving the movement's opponent an excuse to use **repression**."*[322]

*"A local citizen's movement emerged in Santa Lucia Cotzumalguapa [Guatemala] after the civil war to recover the community from drug lords and organized crime, prevent electoral fraud, maintain resilience in the face of violent **repression**, and foster development."*[323]

■ **RELATED TERMS**

oppression, punishment, **repress**, **sanctions** (plural noun), **violence**

126 RESILIENCE

NOUN

The ability of a civil resistance movement or campaign to persist over time, recover from internal or external setbacks, and/or withstand attempts to cause demobilization and disengagement through [violent] repression.

■ **USAGE IN A SENTENCE**

*"In both South Africa and the Philippines, the labor movements were characterized by decentralized structures that provided **resilience** in the face of intense repression."*[324]

*"The coalition devolved leadership to local levels, enhancing **resilience** when the government arrested or killed more prominent leaders."* [325]

■ **RELATED TERMS**
endurance, stamina, steadfastness

127 REVOLUTION
(social, political, or economic)

NOUN

A process, event, or time period in which an existing dominant social, political, and/or economic system is fundamentally changed and replaced with a new system.

■ **COMMENTARY**

The term "revolution" is used in many contexts. In the political context, revolution has been used to refer to anything from violent overthrows of government, to nonviolent movements that created political transitions, to coups d'état that oust a particular leader. In the economic context, the term "revolution" may refer to a radical change in business or the economy (i.e., "The Industrial Revolution"). In the social context, revolution may refer to a radical change in societal values, culture, or customs.

In the field of civil resistance, the term most commonly refers to movements, and/or the impacts of movements, that used nonviolent means to lead to a political transition. For example, the 1986 People Power Movement and the events that it set into motion in the Philippines are often referred to as the "People Power Revolution." The term "Color Revolution" is sometimes applied to a series of popular nonviolent movements (including movements in Serbia [2000], Georgia [2003], and Ukraine [2004]) that ousted various governments. The term "Color Revolution" is also sometimes used as a generic term to refer to revolutions driven by popular nonviolent movements, especially in the 21st century.

Note that a "nonviolent revolution" does not necessarily mean that absolutely no violence occurred in the process of revolution, but rather that the driving force of the revolution was mass nonviolent pressure.

Some scholars (who are not in the field of civil resistance) define revolution as being inherently violent, and some people assume that revolutions must be violent. The French revolution (1789-99), the second Russian revolution (1917), and the Chinese revolution (1946-50) all involved mass violence and shaped perceptions of the term "revolution."

However, the assumption that revolutions must be violent is starting to change as nonviolent movements show that they are able to create revolutions as well, which often lead to different (and more democratic) outcomes than their violent counterparts.

Some scholars also study "revolution from above" by looking at how elites can drive revolutions, but in the field of civil resistance, the term "revolution" refers to mass popular nonviolent action as the driving force. Revolutions are sometimes followed by "counter-revolutions," which are attempts by a previous ruling group to regain power.

■ **USAGE IN A SENTENCE**

*"The 1919 **revolution** [in Egypt] was a genuine people's uprising, largely nonviolent, which was not tainted by religious fanaticism or class conflict, that brought together a coalition of government officials, intellectuals, merchants, peasants, students, and, most remarkably, women."* [326]

*"Georgia's authoritarian government fell in 2003 in a "rose" revolution brought about, at least in part, by three weeks of protests with tens of thousands on the streets. The next year Ukraine's post-Soviet regime came to a similar dramatic end in an "orange" **revolution** involving thousands of Ukrainians camped patiently in the December snow."* [327]

■ **RELATED TERMS**
civilian insurrection, counter-revolution, insurrection, **movement**, rebellion, **uprising**

---

128 SANCTIONS

PLURAL NOUN

Punishments or reprisals imposed because people, institutions, or governments have either:

a. **failed to act in the expected, desired, or legally required manner; or**

b. **acted in an unexpected, undesired, or prohibited manner.**

■ **COMMENTARY**

The scholar Gene Sharp lists the capacity to commit sanctions as one of the six sources of power available to a government or a nonviolent movement. In civil resistance literature, the term "sanctions" is often used in the context of listing Sharp's six sources of power. In this context, sanctions can be violent or nonviolent.

However, the term may also refer to international economic or diplomatic sanctions (as in the second usage example below).

■ **USAGE IN A SENTENCE**

"*[Combatting election fraud in Serbia] NGOs and the local independent media boycotted representatives of the government, thus isolating government supporters through the use of social **sanctions**.*"[328]

"*In the end a concerted grassroots nonviolent civil resistance movement in coalition with international support and **sanctions** forced the white government [of Apartheid South Africa] to negotiate.*"[329]

■ **RELATED TERMS**
punishment, **repression**, reprisal

129 SELF-DETERMINATION

NOUN

The capacity of a population, group, or nation to make binding decisions, which are respected domestically and internationally, about how it shall govern itself.

■ **COMMENTARY**

In civil resistance literature, the term "self-determination" is most often used to refer to struggles for autonomy or secession/independence. For example, the Tibetan people are currently in a self-determination struggle against Chinese rule.

However, the term can also be used more broadly to refer to wthe general right of people to determine their own political future, for example, through a democratic political process.

Regardless of which emphasis is used, there are formal and informal aspects of achieving self-determination. The informal aspect may happen through civil resistance or other forms of political pressure, which lead to a formal process (for example, a direct vote or other political mechanism) to decide on self-determination issues.

"Self-determination" is also a legal concept enshrined in the UN Charter under Article 1, which states: "The Purposes of the United Nations [is] to develop friendly relations among nations based on respect for the principle of equal rights and self-determination of peoples (...)." It is also included in most major international legal instruments, firmly establishing it as a fundamental right in international law. For example, the first article common to the International Covenant on Civil and Political Rights and the International Covenant on Economic, Social and Cultural Rights (1976) provides that "All peoples have the right to self-determination. By virtue of that right they freely determine their political status and freely pursue their economic, social and cultural development."

■ **USAGE IN A SENTENCE**

*"... Indonesian President Suharto ordered the Indonesian military to launch a full-scale invasion of Dili, the East Timorese capital. Close to 60,000 East Timorese were killed or died from starvation or disease in the months following the invasion. Two UN Security Council resolutions, 384 (1975) and 389 (1976), affirmed East Timor's right to **self-determination** and called on Indonesia to halt the invasion and withdraw its military forces without delay."* [330]

*"Until the nine-month-long bloody war that captured the attention of the world and led to the liberation of Bangladesh in December 1971, the struggle for the right to national self-expression and **self-determination** was fought through the use of civil resistance methods and strategies."* [331]

■ **RELATED TERMS**
freedom (political), independence

---

130 SELF-ORGANIZE

VERB

To create order or coordination among members of one's own group, without relying on an external authority (i.e., a government, corporation, or university) or official leader to solve problems or work for their collective good.

Such order or coordination arises out of the will and activity of a group's members making their own decisions, rather than relying on official institutions or the government.

■ **COMMENTARY**

In civil resistance, self-organizing is an important part of the process that leads to the development of a new movement or campaign.

■ **USAGE IN A SENTENCE**

"Movements **self-organize** to summon mass participation, develop cognitive unity in the midst of dissension, and build resilient force on the content of shared beliefs."[332]

■ **RELATED TERMS**

alternative institution, constructive programme, parallel institution, self-rule

131 SELF-ORGANIZATION

NOUN

The process through which people create order or coordination among each other, without relying on an external authority (i.e., a government, corporation, or university) or official leader to tell them what to do.

Such order or coordination arises out of the will and activity of a group's members making their own decisions, rather than relying on official institutions or the government.

■ **COMMENTARY**

In civil resistance, self-organization is part of the process that leads to the development of a new movement or campaign.

■ **USAGE IN A SENTENCE**

"When in 1885 the government ordered all subjects to be taught in German, including religion and Polish-language classes, 60,000 people signed a petition that demanded church (rather than state) oversight of religion classes and teaching of the Polish language. These petitions, together with open public meetings to discuss education policies, were lessons in citizens' **self-organization** to defend the rights to their own language."[333]

"While the major unions generally seek to conduct negotiations and make deals on behalf of their constituencies, these [alternative labor] networks depend on the **self-organization** of people *in an affected area—people who understand that their success depends on the success of everyone involved."* [334]

■ **RELATED TERMS**
alternative institution, constructive programme, parallel institution, self-reliance, self-rule

132 SELF-RELIANCE

NOUN

The capacity of a person or group to independently manage their own affairs, make their own judgments, take care of their own needs, and exercise self-determination and self-sufficiency.

■ **COMMENTARY**

Promoting self-reliance is important for many nonviolent movements. When people are self-reliant, they often feel empowered to take action to make changes in their lives and societies and do not feel that they must wait for others (such as powerful elites) to make change for them.

In addition, economic self-reliance is sometimes important for movements to cultivate, because some nonviolent actions (such as strikes or boycotts) can create challenges for activists (such as loss of income or loss of important goods or services), and movements may need to develop alternative ways to meet these economic and material needs.

■ **USAGE IN A SENTENCE**

*"Arresting leaders and banning their organization are inadequate to end the resistance. Such means of repression [may result in] the decentralization of leadership, increased **self-reliance**, and adherence to nonviolent discipline."* [335]

"[Burmese resistance leader U Ottama] championed the cause of making and wearing pinni, *the native homespun cloth of central Burma.... The* pinni *campaign was part of a constructive program to increase **self-reliance** and indigenous employment while simultaneously reducing dependence on, or contribution to, the colonial power."* [336]

■ **RELATED TERMS**
independence, **self-determination, self-organization, self-rule,** self-sufficiency

133 SELF-RULE

NOUN

A state or situation in which a group, population, or nation governs itself.

■ USAGE IN A SENTENCE

*"Gandhi repeatedly argued that genuine **self-rule** (swaraj) was not simply a matter of the governmental arrangements and the identity of the ruler. Instead, democracy was based upon the inner strength of the society."* [337]

■ RELATED TERMS

self-determination, self-government, **self-organization**, **self-reliance**

134 SEMI-AUTHORITARIAN

ADJECTIVE

Neither fully authoritarian nor fully democratic, but instead displaying some characteristics of both authoritarian and democratic systems.

■ COMMENTARY

Semi-authoritarian governments may display the formal traits and institutions of democracy and allow some degree of political freedom, media freedom, and elections to their citizens, but at the same time have policies and practices that protect powerholders from free, fair and open competition that might threaten their ongoing rule.[338]

A defining characteristic of these regimes is the existence and persistence of mechanisms that strongly inhibit or effectively prevent the transfer of power through elections from the hands of the incumbent leader or party to a new political elite or political organization.[339]

Semi-authoritarian governments are sometimes also referred to as "hybrid regimes."

■ USAGE IN A SENTENCE

*"The new **semi-authoritarian** regimes continue to go through the motions of a democratic process, but they have become masters at stifling electoral competition or at keeping parliaments powerless and judiciary systems cowed."* [340]

*"**Semi-authoritarian** systems are not imperfect democracies struggling toward improvement and consolidation but regimes determined to maintain the appearance of democracy without exposing themselves to the political risks that free competition entails."* [341]

■ **RELATED TERMS**

authoritarianism, **authoritarian rule**, hybrid regime

135 SIT-IN

NOUN

A tactic of civil resistance in which one or more people sit and occupy a place or certain facilities, often until their demands are met. [342]

■ **COMMENTARY**

The objective of a sit-in may be to disrupt the normal activities of a facility and/or those who work in or use the facility. The purpose may also be to establish a new social pattern, such as opening particular facilities (such as restaurants, beaches, or swimming pools) to previously excluded persons. This was a widely publicized method in the U.S. Civil Rights Movement. [343]

The scholar Gene Sharp classifies sit-ins as methods of nonviolent intervention, whereby participants directly disrupt the "normal" state of affairs.

Note that this term can also be used as a verb "to sit in," although more commonly people will use the noun form and refer to "conducting a sit-in," "engaging in a sit-in," or "doing a sit-in."

■ **USAGE IN A SENTENCE**

*"In the very first campaign in Janulsaraj District [Afghanistan], when monitors discovered low-quality bricks were being used to build a school, villagers launched a **sit-in** at the construction site and refused to budge until the company brought in new, higher-quality bricks."* [344]

*"On November 7, [1968] there were mass street demonstrations in Prague, Bratislava, Brno, and other cities. Later that month, tens of thousands of students conducted four-day **sit-ins** at high schools and colleges to protest the occupation [by Soviet troops]."* [345]

■ **RELATED TERMS**
act of or tactic of commission, **blockade** (noun), **nonviolent intervention**, occupation, **protest** (noun), **tactics of concentration**

136 SKILLS
(in the context of civil resistance)

PLURAL NOUN

The abilities of an individual or group to use their knowledge and experience effectively to accomplish a task with a pre-determined goal.

■ **COMMENTARY**

The term "skills" is used in several ways in civil resistance literature, although the meaning is similar in all of them.

First, the term signifies knowledge about activism and organizing, for example: "Workshops on civil resistance aim to build organizing, communications, and strategic planning skills that will increase a movement's chance of success."

Second, the scholar Gene Sharp labels "skills and knowledge" as one of the six sources of political power. A ruler's power is supported by the skills, knowledge, and abilities that are provided by persons and groups in the society (human resources) that are loyal to the ruler. A movement's power is supported by the skills, knowledge, and abilities that each of its members bring to the collective effort.[346] For more information on this second usage, see the commentary for the term **sources of power**, (p. 133).

Third, the term "skills" is sometimes used to generally signify the importance of agency and strategic choice in determining movement outcomes. For example, an author might write: "The skills of a movement are more important in determining its outcome than the structural conditions and challenges in the movement's environment." For more information on this third usage, see the commentary for the terms **agency** (human agency) (p. 20), and **structural conditions** (p. 140).

■ **USAGE IN A SENTENCE**

*"Some suggest that the **skills** involved in waging nonviolent resistance can overcome structural conditions that are assumed to be insurmountable, because the actual act of collective resistance can unfreeze unfavorable conditions and generate political space..."* [347]

*"The set of **skills** that organizers must hone to build an alliance among a diverse constituency will be very useful in a democratic government after the departure of an authoritarian leader."* [348]

■ **RELATED TERMS**
agency, **capacity**, **power**, strategic choice, **training**

---

137 SOURCES OF POWER

PLURAL NOUN
The primary origins of political power.

■ **COMMENTARY**
The civil resistance scholar Gene Sharp (and other scholars in related disciplines) argues that political power ultimately comes from the consent and obedience of the governed. He then identifies six "sources of power," which are:

1. authority (which is closely tied to legitimacy)
2. human resources
3. skills and knowledge
4. intangible factors (i.e., norms, traditions, cultural factors and habitual behaviors)
5. material resources
6. sanctions (here Sharp is referring to the *capacity* to commit violent or nonviolent sanctions)

Each of these sources derives from the actions and beliefs of many people in society. They are closely associated with and dependent upon the acceptance, cooperation, and obedience of the population and the people who work in a society's institutions. With a strong supply of these sources, a ruler or movement will be powerful. As the supply is weakened or severed, a ruler's or movement's power will weaken or collapse.

■ **USAGE IN A SENTENCE**
*"In... struggles against dictatorships, oppressive systems, genocide, coups d'état, and foreign occupations... appropriate strategies all involve efforts to restrict and sever the **sources of power** of the hostile forces."* [349]

*"One of the most important **sources of power** is authority, or legitimacy. The undermining of this source of power was exceptionally*

important in Serbia in October 2000. Without authority, the provision of the other sources of power is unstable."[350]

■ **RELATED TERMS**
authority, **consent** (noun), **legitimacy**, **obedience**, **pillars of support**, **political power**, **power**, **sanctions** (plural noun), **skills**

138 STRATEGIC NONVIOLENT STRUGGLE

NOUN

Deliberately planned, disciplined, and targeted waging of conflict by a movement or campaign using strong forms of nonviolent action, especially against powerful and resourceful opponents who may respond with repression.

■ **COMMENTARY**
Strategic nonviolent struggle is nonviolent struggle that is applied according to a strategic plan.

The term "strategic nonviolent action" is sometimes used as a synonym for "strategic nonviolent struggle," although "strategic nonviolent action" often refers to a shorter-timeframe (i.e., the strategic use of nonviolent action in a particular tactic, rather than an entire struggle).

See also the commentary for the term **strategic plan** (p. 135).

■ **USAGE IN A SENTENCE**
*"The Serbian group Otpor!... had a... difficult time finding a role in the post-Milosevic era. Established specifically as the bulwark for **strategic nonviolent struggle**, [after the democratic transition in Serbia] Otpor! attempted to redefine itself as an environmental and political watchdog organisation."*[351]

*"The Tibetan leadership must free itself from the religious worldview that had shaped the vision of the struggle but also constrained actions in the past, and chart a new path firmly rooted in the tenets and practice of **strategic nonviolent struggle**."*[352]

■ **RELATED TERMS**
civil resistance, **grand strategy**, **methods of nonviolent action**, **nonviolent action**, **nonviolent conflict**, nonviolent insurrection, **nonviolent resistance**, **nonviolent struggle**, **people power**, **political defiance**, strategic nonviolent action, **strategic plan**, **strategy**, **tactic**

139 STRATEGIC PLAN

NOUN

A projected course of action, and associated allocation of resources (i.e., material resources, human resources, time), to enable an individual or group to achieve one or more major goals.

Often, short-term and intermediate goals and sequences of action that contribute to accomplishing the major goal are also identified.

■ COMMENTARY

A "strategic plan" is often the result of a strategic planning process, in which planners identify major goals; analyze their environment, their adversary, and themselves; consider different courses of action to achieve their major goals; develop intermediate goals; and identify steps to help them achieve their intermediate goals, which then lead to their major goals.

A complement to a strategic plan is an operational plan, which is far more detailed and contains concrete, specific tactics and actions, and processes to further the goals laid out by the strategic plan.

■ USAGE IN A SENTENCE

"Participants in nonviolent movements must... make complex decisions about the course their movements should take. A ***strategic plan*** is of central importance in doing this.... [M]ovements gain traction when they plan how civil resistance can be systematically organized and adopted by people in society to achieve targeted and focused goals."[353]

"There is rarely victory for nonviolent movements without a ***strategic plan***. Therefore, an understanding of basic strategic principles as well as tools and techniques to analyze their past and current situation is important as movements develop their strategic plans."[354]

■ RELATED TERMS

grand strategy, plan (noun), **strategic nonviolent struggle, strategy, tactic**

140 STRATEGIZE

VERB

The act or process of considering and deciding on a course of action and allocating the resources necessary to enable an individual or group to achieve one or more major goals. This will often include identifying intermediate goals and sequences of action that will contribute to the accomplishment of the goal.

■ COMMENTARY

See also the terms **strategy** (p. 136), and **strategic plan** (p. 135).

■ USAGE IN A SENTENCE

"Resisting an opponent or occupier violently is seen as the sole option for the downtrodden, short of surrender or inaction. This default thinking about material power often overlooks the fact that ordinary people have historically been able to **strategize** and plan effective individual and group actions that turn their perceived weaknesses into strengths."[355]

"Deciding what tactics to use and how they should be sequenced; developing galvanizing propositions for change based on the aspirations and grievances of the people who the movement aims to represent; planning what individuals and groups to target with tactics and what short-, medium-, and long-term objectives to pursue; and building lines of communication so that coalitions can be negotiated and built are just some of the issues around which nonviolent movements must creatively **strategize**."[356]

■ RELATED TERMS

plan (noun), **plan** (verb), **strategic plan**, **strategy**

141 STRATEGY

NOUN

1. A plan that aims to achieve certain short-, mid-, and/or long-term objectives.
2. A plan for the conduct of a major phase, or campaign, within a conflict. A strategy is the "basic idea of how the struggle of a specific campaign shall develop, and how its separate components shall fit together to contribute most advantageously to achieve its objectives."[357]

■ **COMMENTARY**

Most writers in the field of civil resistance use the first definition of the term "strategy," which is a broad and adaptable definition.

The scholar Gene Sharp often uses the second definition of strategy, which is similar to the first definition, but is more technical. Sharp writes about a four-part framework for analyzing and understanding strategic planning in movements, which involves:

1. Grand strategy (or vision)
2. Strategies (or campaigns)
3. Tactics
4. Methods

These four terms are defined in this glossary, with "grand strategy" serving as the broadest conception of how a movement will evolve, which then progresses sequentially down to the most specific and concrete tasks in the movement, which are called "methods." Thus, when Sharp uses the term "strategy," he is often referring to the second category in his framework, in which strategy operates within the scope of the grand strategy. Tactics and specific methods of action are used in smaller scale operations to implement the strategy for a specific campaign.

■ **USAGE IN A SENTENCE**

*"In 1940 Aung San, then general secretary of the Dobama movement, felt that international assistance was necessary even though the main work for liberation must be done in Burma. His **strategy** depended on a countrywide mass resistance movement against British rule. This, he said, should grow progressively, in the form of a series of local and partial strikes of industrial and rural workers escalating to a general and rent strike, followed by mass demonstrations, people's marches, and eventually mass civil disobedience."*[358] *(illustrates the first definition)*

*"[**Strategy** is the] plan of action for a conflict including when to fight and how to utilize various specific actions to advance the goals of the grand strategy. **Strategy** operates within a grand strategy."*[359] *(illustrates the second definition)*

■ **RELATED TERMS**

grand strategy, **methods of nonviolent action**, **plan** (noun), scheme, stratagem, **strategic plan**, **tactic**

142 STRIKE
(associated with civil resistance)

VERB

1. **To deliberately restrict or suspend work to put pressure on the government to win economic, political, and/or social objectives.**
2. **To deliberately refuse to perform an activity that is required or expected.**

■ **COMMENTARY**

In English, sometimes people use "strike" directly as a verb, for example: "The factory workers struck that day." However, a more common usage in English is to say that workers "go on strike." For example, "The factory workers went on strike that day."

The first definition of the word "strike" is the most commonly used, and means deliberately suspending labor by workers. Sometimes this is also referred to as a "labor strike."

However, the word "strike" also has a more general meaning, which is to stop an expected or required activity. Under this definition, for example, students can strike by refusing to attend school (a school strike) or tenants can strike by refusing to pay rent (a rent strike).

■ **USAGE IN A SENTENCE**

*"The railway workers brought the train system to a halt by **striking** and cutting railway lines and destroying the railway switches; the telegraph workers disrupted communication lines while peasants paralyzed trade in rural goods; both actions affected traffic and communication between and within cities and towns."* [360] *(illustrates the first definition)*

*"2013 began with coal miners in Guajira **striking** for better wages and improved working conditions, followed by miners throughout the country who mobilized to show their guild's importance later in July. These miners protested Colombia's national policy of favoring multinationals over artisanal miners' interests and the potential devastation in their hometowns due to large-scale mining techniques."* [361] *(illustrates the first definition)*

"The vast majority of students at Rangoon University joined the strike and set up a strike committee and strikers' camp at nearby Shwedagon Pagoda. The authorities initially ignored the strike committee's demands and then threatened to fail students who did not participate in their exams. However, the strikers held firm and the authorities were forced to back down and postpone the

exams. This gave time for **striking** students to return to their home areas and transform a strike at a single institution into a national campaign, complete with a national student strike committee."³⁶² (illustrates the second definition)

■ **RELATED TERMS**
act of or tactic of omission, labor strikes, **noncooperation**

143 STRIKE
(associated with civil resistance)

NOUN
1. **A deliberate restriction or suspension of work to put pressure on employers or a government to win economic, political, and/or social objectives.**
2. **A deliberate refusal to perform an activity that is required or expected.**

■ **COMMENTARY**
The first definition of the word "strike" is the most commonly used, and means a deliberate suspension of labor by workers. Sometimes this is also referred to as a "labor strike."

However, the word "strike" also has a more general meaning, which is the act of stopping an expected or required activity. Under this definition, strikes can take different forms, for example, a school strike (refusal by students to attend school) or a rent strike (refusal by tenants to pay rent).

When a large portion of society goes on strike affecting numerous industries and the government it is termed a "general strike."

■ **USAGE IN A SENTENCE**
"The methods of the **strike** involve the refusal to continue economic cooperation through work."³⁶³ (illustrates the first definition)

"While the initial nonviolent action was a long-term sit-in outside of parliament, when the threat of confrontation escalated during a march towards the Presidential Palace, opposition leaders called off the sit-in and instead urged their supporters to engage in a tax **strike** and various other forms of noncooperation."³⁶⁴ (illustrates the second definition)

■ **RELATED TERMS**
act of or tactic of omission, general strike, labor strike, **noncooperation**

144 STRUCTURAL CONDITIONS

PLURAL NOUN

A set of interrelated factors (for example, economic, political, demographic, social/cultural) that compose the environment in which a nonviolent movement exists, and which can impact the movement's emergence and evolution to varying degrees.

■ COMMENTARY

The term "structural conditions" tends to be used in academic literature.

There are debates in the field of civil resistance about the role of structural conditions (also sometimes referred to as "conditions," "structures," or "structural factors") and the role of agency (also sometimes referred to as "skills" or "strategic choice") in determining the emergence, development, and outcomes of civil resistance movements. Examples of structural conditions include a country's economy, political system, education level, demographics, geography, level of internet usage, level of corruption, and many other factors. Over the short term, a civil resistance movement cannot control structural conditions, although over the long term it can sometimes impact or transform them.

In contrast, agency-based factors relate directly to the movement itself, such as the movement's message, strategy, and tactical choices, and a movement often has more immediate control over these factors.

■ USAGE IN A SENTENCE

*"Some suggest that the skills involved in waging nonviolent resistance can overcome **structural conditions** that are assumed to be insurmountable, because the actual act of collective resistance can unfreeze unfavorable conditions and generate political space, and the skillful implementation of methods of nonviolent action can erase decades of fear and apathy and empower a populace."*[365]

"... scholars Erica Chenoweth and Maria Stephan rigorously analyzed 323 violent and nonviolent campaigns that challenged sitting governments between 1900 and 2006. Their groundbreaking findings showed that nonviolent campaigns succeeded 53% of the time versus 26% of the time for violent campaigns. They also found that while state repression and other structural factors can influence a civil resistance campaign's prospects for success (though often by less than is commonly assumed—in the case of violent state repression it only reduced success rates by

*about 35%), they found no **structural conditions** that were determinative of movement outcomes."* [366]

*"Furthermore, civil resistance scholarship has often placed greater emphasis on understanding the role of agency, skills, and strategic choice in shaping movement emergence, trajectories, and outcomes, as opposed to the role of **structural conditions**."* [367]

■ **RELATED TERMS**

conditions, structural factors, structures

---

145 SUCCESS
(associated with civil resistance)

NOUN

The achievement of a party's stated objectives in a conflict.

■ **COMMENTARY**

In civil resistance literature, the noun "success" relates to the achievement of a clearly stated goal (or in some cases multiple goals). For example, if a movement's goal is to get a government to create a new policy, the movement can be regarded as a "success" if it achieves this outcome. If the movement only partially achieves its goal (or if the movement has multiple goals, if it achieves only some of those goals), the movement can be called a "partial success." If the movement fails to achieve any of its stated goals, it is called a "failure."

One of the benefits of defining success (and failure) in this narrow sense is that it allows social scientists to more easily study and compare movements and their outcomes.

Some people object to this narrow definition of success, saying that even if a movement fails to achieve its stated objectives, the movement may succeed at creating other positive effects, and therefore the movement should still be called a "success" and should not be called a "failure." However, note that while a movement may "succeed" (verb) or "be successful" (verb + adjective) at achieving certain positive effects, in order for a movement itself to be called a "success" (noun), the movement must achieve its stated objectives.

Another challenge in defining movement success is that a movement may achieve its stated goals (and thus be labeled a "success") but then shortly thereafter there may be a backlash against the movement that reverses the movement's gains. For example, the

2011 pro-democracy movement in Egypt had a goal of ending the rule of President Hosni Mubarak, and it succeeded in this goal, but it was unable to create a sustainable democratic outcome afterwards.

■ **USAGE IN A SENTENCE**

*"The key factor to **success** [for nonviolent campaigns] is the power that mass, broad-based participation provides for a movement. It turns out that, on average, nonviolent campaigns tend to attract far more participants than their violent counterparts."* [368]

*"The 1881 revolution [in Egypt] relied on the nonviolent coercive pressure of both the military and civilian population. [Opposition leader Ahmad] Orabi gained quick **success** by pursuing demands that were limited and posed no direct threat to the regime or generally to the interest of foreign powers. Successfully mobilizing broad-based support across the social strata, including some political leaders, large and small landowners, and urban guilds around the country, he effectively pressured [viceroy] Tawfik [Pasha] to accept the people's demands."* [369]

■ **RELATED TERMS**

achievement, **goal, objective** (noun)

146 TACTIC

NOUN

A short-term action to achieve a specific objective.

■ **COMMENTARY**

Often in the field of civil resistance, the term "tactics" and "methods of nonviolent action" (or simply "methods") are used synonymously and their definitions are similar. For example, many writers would say that a consumer boycott and a mass demonstration are both methods and tactics. In this interpretation, tactics or methods can be used in an improvised way or as part of a broader strategy.

In contrast, the scholar Gene Sharp distinguishes between the terms "tactics" and "methods," and he includes tactics in his four-part framework for analyzing and understanding strategic planning in movements. For Sharp, tactics are always part of a larger strategy. His framework includes:

1. Grand strategy (or vision)
2. Strategies (or campaigns)
3. Tactics
4. Methods

These four terms are defined in this glossary, with "grand strategy" serving as the broadest concept of how a movement will evolve. Campaigns aim to achieve major intermediate objectives that directly support the grand strategy. Each tactic and method aims to achieve short-term objectives that directly support a campaign.

In Sharp's writings, a "tactic" refers to *how* and *why* a particular "method" is applied. For example, Sharp considers a mass demonstration to be a "method," and a "tactic" would relate to the purpose for which the method is employed (for example, to draw attention to corrupt officials) and the manner in which the mass demonstration is held, for example on a certain day, in a certain location, with a certain message, and with certain people who can best convey the movement's message.

However, as stated, most writers have not adopted such a detailed and specific approach as Sharp, and some writers take Sharp's four-part classification (of grand strategy, strategies, tactics, and methods) and reduce it to a three-part classification (of grand strategy, strategies, and methods) by merging the concepts of methods and tactics into the single category of "tactics."

■ **USAGE IN A SENTENCE**
"Using a variety of tactics keeps your opponent off balance and ensures that your opponent can not predict your movement's next action. **Tactics** *should be directly linked to intermediate goals which in turn flow from the movement's or campaign's grand strategy."* [370]

*"***Tactics*** *deal with how particular methods of action… are applied, or how particular groups of combatants shall act in a specific situation."* [371]

■ **RELATED TERMS**
action, **act of or tactic of commission**, **act of or tactic of omission**, **campaign** (noun), **grand strategy**, maneuvers, **methods of nonviolent action**, moves, **tactics of concentration**, **tactics of dispersion**

147 TACTICAL INNOVATION

NOUN

The act of shifting to new tactics and methods of civil resistance, and/or the act of performing previously-used tactics or methods of civil resistance in new ways.

■ **COMMENTARY**

Tactical innovation is a key attribute of many successful civil resistance campaigns and movements. Movements may develop a sequence of tactics that shift over time, for example, a protest, leading to a labor strike, leading to a boycott. Or a movement may perform the same tactics but in a different way, for example, protesting at night, during the day, in different locations, for different durations of time, with large numbers of people, with small numbers of people, etc.

One reason why tactical innovation is important for movements is because opponents learn and adapt to a movement's tactics over time. A civil resistance movement that is able to shift its tactics is able to maintain the initiative, force its opponent to react, and often find new points of leverage.

■ **USAGE IN A SENTENCE**

"Though not often considered part of the nonviolent tactical repertoire, education, training and youth recreation can be vital to build campaign capacity, confidence and resilience. ***Tactical innovation****, such as turning everyday actions into acts of resistance, can thus be crucial to build support, overcome repression... [and] human rights abuses, and maintain campaign resilience."* [372]

"The combination of legitimacy, ***tactical innovation****, and resilience sustains a movement, eventually chipping away at the loyalty within the pillars of support that are propping up an oppressive political institution"* [373]

■ **RELATED TERMS**

escalation, methods of nonviolent action, strategy, tactic, tactical innovation

148 TACTICAL SEQUENCING
(or "sequencing of tactics")

NOUN

A planned progression of nonviolent tactics, with the aim of achieving a goal, often by escalating pressure on a movement's opponent.

■ **COMMENTARY**

Strategic planning in civil resistance often involves developing sequences of tactics to increase the intensity and range of ways that the movement can pressure its opponent. Because tactics often change throughout a sequence, tactical sequencing and tactical innovation are often related.

■ **USAGE IN A SENTENCE**

"The social accountability field can benefit from accumulated knowledge about effective social movements, particularly the need for strategy, planning, organization and **tactical sequencing**, innovation, and diversity." [374]

"**Sequencing [of] tactics** allows your movement to increase pressure on your opponent and to maintain momentum." [375]

■ **RELATED TERMS**

escalation, methods of nonviolent action, strategy, tactic, tactical innovation

149 TACTIC OF CONCENTRATION

PLURAL NOUN

See the term **concentration, tactic of** (p. 41).

150 TACTIC OF DISPERSION

PLURAL NOUN

See the term **dispersion, tactic of** (p. 56).

151 THIRD PARTY
(or "third-party")

NOUN

A group, community, organization, institution, entity, or occasionally a prominent individual, that is not directly engaged at the center of a conflict or struggle, but that takes (or can take) actions that have an impact on the conflict.

■ **COMMENTARY**

Third parties may include: states; multilateral institutions (such as the UN, AU, EU, ASEAN); nongovernmental organizations (NGOs); corporations; external funders of various kinds; diaspora communities; media outlets; foreign civil society groups (i.e., church or student groups); transnational civil resistance movements and campaigns; and highly visible, influential, powerful, and wealthy individuals.

The term "third party" is similar in meaning to the term "external actor." However, the term "third party" is a little broader, because it can include actors *within* the territory or country where a struggle is being waged as well as actors that are *external* to that territory or country. In contrast, the term "external actor" tends to refer only to parties that are based outside of the territory or country where a struggle is being waged (even if, like the UN, they may have an office within the particular territory or country).

■ **USAGE IN A SENTENCE**

"The **third parties** are those not directly involved in the struggle: the general public and most people in other countries. People can move from being a third party to being an activist, and the other way around, as a consequence of actions."[376]

"... all peacebuilders share a common self-identification as impartial **third parties.** They do not belong to, nor associate themselves with, the primary conflict parties."[377]

■ **RELATED TERMS**
ally (noun), **external actor, third party**

---

152 TRAIN

VERB

To teach relevant (often practical) knowledge and/or impart the skills that are needed for an art, profession, or job.

■ **COMMENTARY**

In civil resistance, training helps to build the skills and capacity of a movement's supporters, as well as build trust and cohesion within a movement. It may be part of the movement's recruitment process, although training can be valuable at all phases of involvement in a movement, and at different phases of the movement itself.

See also the commentary for the term **training** (noun) (p. 147).

■ **USAGE IN A SENTENCE**

"It is said that Gandhi **trained** 100,000 Indians in his campaign against British colonialism. Such training was crucial in the black power civil rights movement in the U.S. It had a prominent place in the movement against the war in Vietnam. More recently, it *played a vital role in the 'People Power' movement, which overthrew the Marcos dictatorship in the Philippines."* [378]

"In 1942, radical pacifists formed the 'Nonviolent Action Committee of the Fellowship of Reconciliation,' which **trained** *teams to provide leadership in anti-racist and antimilitarist work. From this group grew the Congress of Racial Equality (CORE) which, in 1945 became the first organisation to develop nonviolence trainings in preparation for involvement in nonviolent actions to desegregate."* [379]

"IWA [Integrity Watch Afghanistan] **trained** *the local [anti-corruption] monitors, providing skills, standards, and tools for monitoring, conducting site inspections, and so on. The volunteers also signed a code of conduct outlining the way they would execute their work and underscoring their commitment to the community to report findings regularly, refuse bribes, and maintain integrity."* [380]

■ **RELATED TERMS**
capacity building, **skills, training**

---

153 TRAINING

NOUN

An event, method or process through which a person or group acquires relevant (often practical) knowledge, skills or experience that are needed for an art, profession, or job.

■ **COMMENTARY**

Training can refer to a time-limited event with a clear goal (such as a workshop that aims to develop certain skills or teach certain knowledge). For example: "I am attending a 2-day training." Training can also refer to a process that takes place over a longer period of time and involves both formal and informal experiences. For example: "My training took place over several years."

In civil resistance, training can be valuable at all phases of involvement in a movement, and at different phases of the movement itself. It helps to build the skills and capacity of a movement's supporters, as well as build trust and cohesion within a movement. It may also be part of the movement's recruitment process.

■ **USAGE IN A SENTENCE**

"The history of **training** *is a history of playing catch-up. Very few movements seem to realize that the pace of change can*

accelerate so rapidly that it outstrips the movement's ability to use its opportunities fully." [381]

*"Every individual in [the Serbian nonviolent movement] Otpor! acted as a transmitter of knowledge, in large part because of the systematic skills **training** all members had received for a period of more than two years."* [382]

■ **RELATED TERMS**
capacity, capacity building, **skills**, **train** (verb)

154 TRANSITION, POLITICAL

NOUN

1. A change in political ruler and regime.
2. The time period between two forms of stable political rule; when one form of political rule has ended and a new form of stable political rule is developing.[383]

■ **COMMENTARY**
Civil resistance movements may drive political transitions by pushing for authoritarian or semi-authoritarian governments to become democratic—for example, by forcing an autocrat to resign or to acknowledge defeat in elections that the autocrat tried to steal. When a political transition results in democracy, it is often termed a "democratic transition."

However, it is notable that not all political transitions driven by pro-democracy movements result in democracy. Sometimes a civil resistance movement will achieve a political transition but then the resulting transition process leads to a new authoritarian or semi-authoritarian government. In this regard, political transitions "from" authoritarianism are not always the same as political transitions "to" democracy.

Some people use the term "regime change" to describe political transitions, and indeed, the terms have similar literal meanings. However, the term "regime change" is sometimes associated with external intervention, particularly armed intervention and foreign-backed coups d'état, and therefore it is not a term that is well-suited to use with civil resistance movements.

■ **USAGE IN A SENTENCE**
*"The proliferation and success of such civic resistance movements in effecting **political transitions** is spawning increased*

international discussion of the mechanisms by which democracy replaces tyranny." [384] *(illustrates the first definition)*

*"... nonviolent resistance—and, with that, the agency of ordinary people—has played a crucial role in dozens of major **political transitions** over the last several decades. Some examples are the anti-colonial struggles of the 1960s, the struggles against military rule in Latin America in the 1980s, the anti-Communist movements of 1989-1991, the color revolutions of the early 2000s, and the Arab Spring movements of 2010-12."* [385] *(illustrates the first definition)*

*"The first... challenge [in moving from non-democratic rule towards democracy] is continued mobilization of ordinary people during the **political transition**. Initiating a political transition through nonviolent resistance means that large numbers of people have mobilized to push for political change. Yet keeping these large numbers of people politically engaged in the process of building a new political regime after a successful nonviolent resistance campaign can be extremely difficult."* [386] *(illustrates the second definition)*

■ **RELATED TERMS**
coup d'état, democratic transition, election, regime change, **revolution**

155 UNARMED INSURRECTION

NOUN

See the term **insurrection, unarmed** (p. 78).

156 UNITE

VERB

To join together for a common purpose, goal, or action.

■ **COMMENTARY**
Many populations that are oppressed have been subject to a "divide and rule" strategy by their oppressor. This strategy aims to break down trust, contact, and unity among different groups, so that they can be ruled/oppressed more easily. In some cases, oppressors are successful in creating conflict among different groups so that the groups become focused on each other instead of uniting to challenge their oppressor.

Therefore, in order to be effective, nonviolent movements often must unite different groups who normally do not work together to take collective action to pursue shared goals.

See also the commentary for the term **unity** (p. 150).

■ **USAGE IN A SENTENCE**

*"[Brazilian anti-corruption] mobilizations are **uniting** citizens from different walks of life and civic organizations, and [people] are identifying linkages between corruption, poverty, violence, and democracy."* [387]

*"The nonviolent language movements of 1948 and 1952 earned Bangla its due recognition as one of the state languages of Pakistan. More importantly, these movements helped **unite** Bengalis by defining and strengthening their national consciousness and identity. This development of linguistically and culturally based nationalism, according to a number of Bengali scholars, laid the foundation for the creation of a nation-state."* [388]

■ **RELATED TERMS**
coalition, coalition building, **unity**

---

157 UNITY

NOUN

The state of being united or joined together for a common purpose, goal, or action.

■ **COMMENTARY**

Unity is key for the success of a nonviolent movement. However, it is notable that there are different aspects of this concept:

- "Unity of purpose" means uniting diverse people around a common goal.
- "Unity of organization" means unity among people at all levels of leadership.
- "Unity of a people" means diverse groups have come together from a wider population to work together.

To achieve these different forms of unity, movements often must develop a "unifying vision" (which draws on shared goals and grievances of various groups) of what the movement wants to achieve together. Movements may also try to create unity through training programs that bring different groups together, and through deliberate actions where one group shows solidarity and supports another group.

See also the commentary for the term **unite** (p. 149).

- **USAGE IN A SENTENCE**

"The effectiveness of nonviolent action increases when the resisters and the general grievance group possess a high degree of internal **unity**."[389]

"For example, the South African anti-apartheid movement's ongoing civic disruption combined with its call for national reconciliation was able to garner widespread support and create **unity** for the cause of change, even among some white supporters who had previously supported the apartheid state."[390]

- **RELATED TERMS**

coalition, coalition building, unifying vision, **unite**

158 UPRISING

NOUN

A revolt or rebellion by a group or population that previously submitted to a government or status quo.[391]

- **COMMENTARY**

Uprisings may be planned or spontaneous. They may involve the use of violence, civil resistance, or a combination of both.

Regarding civil resistance, an uprising may be organized by an existing movement. Or an uprising may be a short-term spontaneous revolt that does not result in the creation of a new movement or any long-term change. Or an uprising may start as a spontaneous revolt, persist over time, and lead to the development of a new movement.

- **USAGE IN A SENTENCE**

"In extreme cases, such as a nonviolent **uprising** to end an extreme dictatorship, success may be produced by the... [dissolution] of the oppressive system."[392]

"Paramilitary, guerrilla, or other **uprisings** are directed against a state from within in order to achieve political objectives."[393]

- **RELATED TERMS**

insubordination, insurgency, insurrection, resistance, revolt

159 VIOLENCE

NOUN

1. **Direct or threatened infliction of physical harm on some individuals by other individuals.**[394]
2. **"The intentional use of physical force or power, threatened or actual, against oneself, another person, or against a group or community, which either results in or has a high likelihood of resulting in injury, death, psychological harm, maldevelopment, or deprivation."**[395]

■ **COMMENTARY**

The first definition of violence is the most common definition used in the field of civil resistance. The definition of "nonviolent action"—and related terms such as "civil resistance," "nonviolent conflict" and "nonviolent struggle"—all use the first definition of violence to show the kind of action that is excluded under their respective definitions.

The scholar Gene Sharp also notes that under the first definition, "Violence, therefore, includes imprisonment, because it is maintained by infliction or threat of physical harm in case of attempted escape."[396]

There is sometimes disagreement under the first definition about whether "violence" includes acts that are harmful to oneself—for example, some argue that a hunger strike is violent if the hunger striker dies, or argue that self-immolation is violent. Others say that these are nonviolent acts because they are not using or threatening to use physical violence on others.

The second definition of violence is broader than the first definition, and is used in a variety of other fields (outside of civil resistance), and encompasses psychological violence and structural violence. Structural violence, such as poverty or racism, refers to the conditions (structures) in an individual's environment that prevent them from fulfilling their fundamental needs as a human being, and therefore damage them or are likely to result in some kind of damage or violence to them. Therefore, in the field of civil resistance, this second definition of violence may be used to refer to grievances and systems of oppression that activists and societies face.

■ **USAGE IN A SENTENCE**

*"The decline in the effectiveness of **violence** is easily explained by the decline of state sponsorship for violent insurgencies, which is largely a function of the end of the Cold War."* [397]

*"When nonviolent protagonists maintain discipline, they not only delegitimize the opponents' **violence**, but they also gain credibility, stature, and, ultimately, power."* [398]

■ **RELATED TERMS**
agent provocateur, repression, violent flank

160 VIOLENT FLANK

NOUN

An armed group that uses violence and/or property destruction to pursue their goals, and wages conflict contemporaneously with a nonviolent movement.

■ **COMMENTARY**

A violent flank may be a wing within an otherwise nonviolent movement (an "intra-movement violent flank"), or it may be fully external to a nonviolent movement (an "extra-movement violent flank").[399] It can have similar, or significantly different, grievances and objectives than the nonviolent movement.

Some scholars write about a "violent flank effect," which refers to impacts that the presence of violent flanks has on nonviolent movements.[400]

Violent flanks are sometimes referred to as "radical flanks." However, the term "violent flank" is more appropriate for this definition, since people may have radical political views but not approve of violence. Therefore, the term "radical flank" falsely equates radicalism with violence, and thus hopefully will fall out of use in the English language. Furthermore, it can be argued that civil resistance is in fact a *more* radical method of action than violence. For example, commenting on pro-democracy movements in Soviet-controlled Europe in the 1970s, dissident Vaclav Havel wrote: "The 'dissident' movements do not shy away from the idea of violent political overthrow because the idea seems too radical, but on the contrary, because it does not seem radical enough."[401]

■ **USAGE IN A SENTENCE**

*"...many states would prefer, strategically, to face armed movements rather than unarmed ones. **Violent flanks** allow the*

government to justify using repression—against unarmed protesters as well as armed ones. And in general, governments are going to win at that game, particularly if the repression drives even more participants away."[402]

"A simple model estimating the effects of **violent flanks** on campaign participation reveals that **violent flanks** substantially reduce the number of participants in unarmed struggle."[403]

■ **RELATED TERMS**
radical flank, violent (or radical) flank effect, violent insurgency

161 VISION
(of a civil resistance movement)

NOUN

An articulation and/or expression of the ultimate goals of a movement, describing the future of the community or society that the movement wishes to achieve.

■ **COMMENTARY**

A movement's vision can include statements and/or symbols of what the movement stands for and against. The goals and objectives within the vision are often general (such as "we will have a fully functioning democracy" or "people will rise out of poverty"), although there may be some specific goals included as well (i.e., "we will adopt a particular policy or Constitutional amendment"). An effective vision unifies people and is a reference point in determining which intermediate and short-term objectives to pursue in order to advance the vision.

A movement's vision can be considered a part of its "grand strategy." The vision is sometimes also called a "vision of tomorrow."

■ **USAGE IN A SENTENCE**

"[The Indian anti-corruption movement] 5th Pillar's **vision** is, quite simply, to realize freedom from corruption. The struggle is viewed as a continuation of the Indian independence movement."[404]

"Together, we demand an end to the wars against Black people. We demand that the government repair the harms that have been done to Black communities in the form of reparations and targeted long-term investments. We also demand a defunding of the systems and institutions that criminalize and cage us. This document articulates our **vision** of a fundamentally different world."[405]

■ **RELATED TERMS**
goal, **grand strategy**, **plan** (verb), vision of tomorrow

---

162 WALK OUT

VERB

To protest or express disapproval by physically leaving a place of work, meeting, assembly, event, company, or organization before a regularly expected time. The departure is usually made in an obvious way so that visibility of the action is maximized.[406]

■ **USAGE IN A SENTENCE**
At [Pakistani President Jinnah's speech on March 18, 1948]... at Dhaka University, some students **walked out** while others shouted until he abandoned his speech and left the premises.[407]

■ **RELATED TERMS**
boycott of institutions, labor strike, **noncooperation**, **strike** (verb)

---

163 WALK-OUT
(or "walkout")

NOUN

An expression of protest or disapproval by physically leaving a place of work, meeting, assembly, event, company, or organization before a regularly expected time. The departure is usually made in an obvious way so that visibility of the action is maximized.[408]

■ **USAGE IN A SENTENCE**
"Government officials... staged a **walkout** and soon were joined by workers and officials of the East Bengal Railway."[409]

"A youth-led activists group in Baltimore City has planned a district wide student **walkout** on Friday to protest standardized testing, which they call a mechanism of institutional racism."[410]

■ **RELATED TERMS**
boycott of institutions, labor strike, **noncooperation**, **strike** (noun)

Translations of Key Terms

As of January 2021 many of the terms contained in this glossary have been translated into:

Arabic	Kannada	Russian
Armenian	Khmer	Sindhi
Bahasa Indonesia	Kirundi	Spanish
Bangla	Kiswahili	Tamil
Chinese	Kyrgyz	Telugu
Creole (Haitian)	Malayalam	Thai
Farsi (Persian)	Pashto	Turkish
Filipino/Tagalog	Polish	Urdu
French	Portuguese (Brazilian)	Vietnamese
Hebrew		
Hindi	Portuguese (Continental)	
Hungarian		

Often these translated key terms were developed based on earlier drafts of this glossary, and commissioned by the International Center on Nonviolent Conflict (ICNC).

You can find these translated terms at:
https://www.nonviolent-conflict.org/translations

Endnotes

1. Smolar, Aleksander. "Towards 'Self-Limiting Resolution': Poland 1970-89." *Civil Resistance and Power Politics: The Experience of Non-Violent Action from Gandhi to the Present*, edited by Adam Roberts and Timothy Garton Ash, Oxford University Press, 2012, p. 133.

2. Merriman, Hardy. "Theory and Dynamics of Nonviolent Action." *Civilian Jihad Nonviolent Struggle, Democratization, and Governance in the Middle East*, edited by Maria J. Stephan, Palgrave Macmillan, 2010, p. 23.

3. Miller, Christopher E. *Only Young Once: An Introduction to Nonviolent Struggle for Youths*. Addis Ababa: U for Peace, Africa Programme, 2006. Print, p. 22.

4. Based on: Sharp, Gene. *Waging Nonviolent Struggle: 20th Century Practice and 21st Century Potential*. Boston: Porter Sargent Publishers, 2005, p. 543 with significant modification by the authors.

5. Lakey, G. (1968). "The Sociological Mechanisms of Nonviolent Action." *Peace Research Review* 2(6): 1–102.

6. Dudouet, Véronique. *Nonviolent Resistance and Conflict Transformation in Power Asymmetries*. Berlin: Berghof Research Center for Constructive Conflict Management, 2008. Print, p. 16.

7. Sharp, Gene. *Self-Liberation: A Guide to Strategic Planning for Action to End a Dictatorship or Other Oppression*. East Boston: Albert Einstein Institution, 2010, p. 46.

8. Popovic, Srdja, et al. *CANVAS Core Curriculum: A Guide to Effective Nonviolent Struggle*. Belgrade: Centre for Applied Nonviolent Action and Strategies, 2007, p. 59.

9. Based on (with minor variation): Snodderly, Dan, ed. *Peace Terms: Glossary of Terms for Conflict Management and Peacebuilding*. Washington: Endowment of the United States Institute of Peace, 2011. Web, p. 9.

10. Ibid.

11. Beyerle, Shaazka. *Curtailing Corruption: People Power for Accountability and Justice*. Boulder: Lynne Rienner Publishers, 2014. Print, p. 56.

12. Beyerle, Shaazka. "Civil Resistance and the Corruption - Violence Nexus." *Journal of Sociology and Social Welfare* 38.2 (2012): 53-77. Print, p. 69.

13. Based on: Sharp, Gene, et al. *Sharp's Dictionary of Power and Struggle: Language of Civil Resistance in Conflicts*. New York: Oxford UP, 2012. p. 54.

14. Pinckney, Jonathan. *Making or Breaking Nonviolent Discipline in Civil Resistance Movements*, ICNC Press, 2016, p. 49.

15. Principe, Marie A. *Women in Nonviolent Movements*. United States Institute of Peace, Special Report, no. 399, 2017, p. 9.

16. Ackerman, Peter and, Shaazka Beyerle (2016). "Lessons from Civil Resistance for the Battle against Financial Corruption." *Diogenes*, 61(3–4), p. 82–96.

17. DuVall, Jack (2014). "Dream Things True: Nonviolent Movements as Applied Consciousness." *Cosmos and History: The Journal of Natural and Social Philosophy*, 10(1), p. 106.

18. Bartkowski, Maciej J. "Insights into Nonviolent Liberation Struggles." *Recovering Nonviolent History: Civil Resistance in Liberation Struggles*. Boulder: Lynne Rienner, 2013. Print, p. 344.

19. Ibid.

20. Based on: Sharp, *Dictionary*, p. 55.

21. Miller, Christopher. "Defending Democracy in Thailand - 1992." *Waging Nonviolent Struggle: 20th Century Practice and 21st Century Potential*. By Gene Sharp. Boston: Extending Horizons, 2005. Print, p. 308.

22. Sharp, Gene. *Waging Nonviolent Struggle: 20th Century Practice and 21st Century Potential*. Boston: Extending Horizons, 2005. Print, p. 353.

23. Stephan, Maria J. and Erica Chenoweth. "Why Civil Resistance Works: The Strategic Logic of Nonviolent Conflict." *International Security*, vol. 33, no. 1, 2008, p. 36.

24. Lakey, George. "Know Your Allies, Your Opponents and Everyone in Between." *wagingnonviolence.org*, 27 July 2012.

25. Based on: New Tactics in Human Rights, comp. "Key Terms for Understanding New Tactics' Strategic Effectiveness Method." 2010. Web.

26. Bartkowski, Maciej J. "Insights into Nonviolent Liberation Struggles." *Recovering Nonviolent History: Civil Resistance in Liberation Struggles*. Boulder: Lynne Rienner, 2013. Print, p. 344.

27. Crist, John T., Harriet Hentges, and Daniel Serwer. *Strategic Nonviolent Conflict Lessons from the Past, Ideas for the Future*. Special Report. United States Institute of Peace. Washington: 2002. Web, p. 5.

28. Zunes, Stephen, Lester R. Kurtz, and Sarah Beth Asher. *Nonviolent Social Movements: A Geographical Perspective*. Malden: Blackwell, 1999. Print.

29. Bartkowski, Maciej J. "Recovering Nonviolent History." *Recovering Nonviolent History: Civil Resistance in Liberation Struggles*. Boulder: Lynne Rienner, 2013. Print, p. 18.

30. Moser-Puangsuwan, Yeshua. "Burma: Civil Resistance in the Anticolonial Struggle, 1910s-1940." in Maciej J. Bartkowski (ed.). *Recovering Nonviolent History: Civil Resistance in Liberation Struggles*. Boulder: Lynne Rienner, 2011. Print, p. 194.

31. Sharp, Gene and Bruce Jenkins. *The Anti-Coup*. Boston: Albert Einstein Institution, 2003. Print, p. 16.

32. Based on: Sharp, *Dictionary*, p. 65-66.

33. Sharp, Gene. *Waging Nonviolent Struggle: 20th Century Practice and 21st Century Potential*. Boston: Extending Horizons, 2005. Print, p. 31.

34. Paulson, Joshua. "Removing the Dictator in Serbia—1996-2000" in Sharp, Gene. *Waging Nonviolent Struggle*. p. 319.

35. *New Oxford American Dictionary*.

36. Martin, Brian. *Backfire Manual*. Sparsnäs: Irene, 2012. Print.

37. Schock, Kurt. *Civil Resistance Today*. Cambridge: Polity, 2015. Print, p. 16.

38. Nepstad, Sharon Erickson. *Nonviolent Struggle: Theories, Strategies, Dynamics*. New York: Oxford University Press, 2015. Print, p. 127.

39. Based on: Sharp, *Dictionary*, p. 67.

40. Bartkowski, Maciej J. "Insights into Nonviolent Liberation Struggles." *Recovering Nonviolent History: Civil Resistance in Liberation Struggles*. Boulder: Lynne Rienner, 2013. Print, p. 348.

41. Kurtz, Lester. "The Mothers of the Disappeared: Challenging the Junta in Argentina (1977 – 1983)." International Center on Nonviolent Conflict (2010): 1-10., p. 3.

42. Huq, Aziz. "This Is How Democratic Backsliding Begins." *Vox*. 15 May 2017. Web.

43. Moser-Puangsuwan, Yeshua. "Burma: Civil Resistance in the Anticolonial Struggle, 1910s-1940." In Maciej J. Bartkowski (ed.). *Recovering Nonviolent History: Civil Resistance in Liberation Struggles*. Boulder: Lynne Rienner, 2011. Print, p. 190.

44. Smedjeback, Martin. "Forms of Nonviolent Action." In *Handbook for Nonviolent Campaigns*, Second Edition, edited by Gárate, Javier, et al. London: War Resisters' International, 2014, p. 125.

45. Kurtz, Lester. "Otpor and the Struggle for Democracy in Serbia (1998-2000)." International Center on Nonviolent Conflict, 2010.

46. Beyerle, Shaazka. *Curtailing Corruption: People Power for Accountability and Justice*. Boulder: Lynne Rienner Publishers, 2014. Print, p. 225.

47. Cortright, David. *Gandhi and Beyond: Nonviolence for a New Political Age*. Boulder: Paradigm, 2009. Print, p. 92.

48. Conser, Jr., Walter H. "The United States: Reconsidering the Struggle for Independence, 1765–1775" in Maciej Bartkowski, *Recovering Nonviolent History: Civil Resistance in Liberation Struggles*. Boulder: Lynne Rienner, 2013. Print, p. 344.

49 Powers, Roger S., William B. Vogele, Christopher Kruegler, and Ronald M. McCarthy (eds.). *Protest, Power, and Change: An Encyclopedia of Nonviolent Action from ACT-UP to Women's Suffrage*. New York and London: Garland Publishing, Inc. 1997. Print. p. 51.

50 Mogul, Jonathan. *A Force More Powerful: Study Guide*. Ed. Barbara De Boinville. Potomac: Toby Levine Communications, 2000. Print, p. 6.

51 Sharp, *Waging Nonviolent Struggle*, p. 159.

52 *New Oxford American Dictionary*.

53 Momba, Jotham C. and Fay Gadsen. "Zambia: Nonviolent Strategies Against Colonialism, 1900s–1960s." in Maciej J. Bartkowski (ed.). *Recovering Nonviolent History: Civil Resistance in Liberation Struggles*. Boulder: Lynne Rienner, 2011. Print, p. 77.

54 Ishtiaq, Hossain. "Bangladesh: Civil Resistance in the Struggle for Independence, 1948–1971." in Maciej J. Bartkowski (ed.). *Recovering Nonviolent History: Civil Resistance in Liberation Struggles*. Boulder: Lynne Rienner, 2011. Print, p. 208.

55 Stephan, Maria J. and Erica Chenoweth. "Why Civil Resistance Works: The Strategic Logic of Nonviolent Conflict." *International Security*, vol. 33, no. 1, 2008, p. 8.

56 Based on: Sharp, *Dictionary*, p. 74.

57 Stoner, Eric. "Participation Is Everything - a Conversation with Erica Chenoweth." *Waging Nonviolence*. 14 July 2012. Web.

58 Sharp, Gene. *How Nonviolent Struggle Works*. Boston: Albert Einstein Institute, 2013. Print, p. 131.

59 Snodderly, *Peace Terms*, p. 24.

60 Ackerman, Peter, and Hardy Merriman. "A Checklist for Ending Tyranny." *Is Authoritarianism Staging a Comeback?* Matthew Burrows and Maria J. Stephan (eds.). Washington, DC: Atlantic Council, 2015. 63-80. Print.

61 Ibid.

62 Based on: Sharp, Gene. *From Dictatorship to Democracy: A Conceptual Framework for Liberation*. New York: New, 2012. Print, p. 32.

63 Thoreau, "Civil Disobedience," New York Washington Square Press, 1968. This essay is sometimes also referred to by the title "On Civil Disobedience" and "On the Duty of Civil Disobedience."

64 Mogul, *A Force More Powerful Study Guide*, p. 4.

65 Schock, Kurt. *Unarmed Insurrections: People Power Movements in Nondemocracies*. Minneapolis: University of Minnesota, 2005. Print, p. 57.

66 Based on the definition of "nonviolent action" in Sharp. *Waging Nonviolent Struggle: 20th Century Practice and 21st Century Potential*. Boston: Extending Horizons, 2005. Print, p. 41.

67 Ackerman, Peter. "Skills or Conditions: What Key Factors Shape the Success or Failure of Civil Resistance?" Conference on Civil Resistance and Power Politics, 15 Mar. 2007.

68 Ibid.

69 Bartkowski, Maciej. "Recovering Nonviolent History" in Maciej J. Bartkowski (ed.). *Recovering Nonviolent History: Civil Resistance in Liberation Struggles*. Boulder: Lynne Rienner, 2011. Print, p. 24.

70 Schock, *Unarmed Insurrections*, p. 119.

71 Based on: Sharp, *Dictionary*, p. 83.

72 Sharp, *Waging Nonviolent Struggle*, p. 515.

73 Holst, Johan Jørgen. *Civilian-Based Defense in a New Era*. Cambridge: Albert Einstein Institution, 1990. Print, p. 21.

74 Chenoweth and Stephan, *Why Civil Resistance Works*.

75 Beyerle, *Curtailing Corruption*, p. 107.

76 Bartkowski, Maciej. "Appendix: Conflict Summaries." in Maciej Bartkowski (ed.). *Recovering Nonviolent History: Civil Resistance in Liberation Struggles*. Boulder: Lynne Rienner, 2011. Print, p. 372.

77 Based on: Sharp, *Dictionary*, p. 193.

78 Dorjee, Tenzin. *The Tibetan Nonviolent Struggle: A Strategic and Historical Analysis*. ICNC Monograph Series. Washington, DC: ICNC Press, 2015. Print, p. 12.

79 Schock, *Unarmed Insurrection*, p. 51.

80 "Tactics of Concentration and Dispersion." *Tibet Action Institute*, 14 Dec. 2015. Web.

81 Based on: Sharp, *Dictionary*, p. 96.

82 Based on: Sharp, *Dictionary*, p. 96.

83 Mogul, *A Force More Powerful Study Guide*, p. 2.

84 Schock, Kurt. "Nonviolent Action and Its Misconceptions: Insights for Social Scientists." *PS: Political Science and Politics* 36.4 (2003): 705-12. JSTOR. Web, p. 705.

85 *New Oxford American Dictionary*.

86 Sharp, Gene. *Gandhi as a Political Strategist, with Essays on Ethics and Politics*. Cambridge, Massachusetts: Porter Sargent, 1979, p. 14–15.

87 Miller, Christopher E. *Only Young Once: An Introduction to Nonviolent Struggle for Youths*. Addis Ababa: U for Peace, Africa Programme, 2006. Print, p. 28.

88 Drake, Denise and Steve Whiting. "Working in Groups." In *Handbook for Nonviolent Campaigns*, Second Edition, edited by Gárate, Javier, et al. London: War Resisters' International, 2014, p. 99.

89 Bill Moyer, *Doing Democracy*, Gabriola Island, BC: New Society Publishers, 2001. Print. p. 12

90 Sharp, *How Nonviolent Struggle Works*, p. 82.

91 Sharp, *Dictionary*, p. 100.

92 Sheehan, Joanne, et al. "Constructive programme." In *Handbook for Nonviolent Campaigns*, Second Edition, edited by Gárate, Javier, et al. London: War Resisters' International, 2014, p. 56.

93 Dudouet, *Nonviolent Resistance and Conflict Transformation in Power Asymmetries*, p. 14.

94 Based on: Sharp, *There are Realistic Alternatives*, p. 32.

95 Lakey, G. (1968). "The Sociological Mechanisms of Nonviolent Action." *Peace Research Review* 2(6): 1–102.

96 Popovic, et al. *CANVAS Core Curriculum: A Guide to Effective Nonviolent Struggle*, p. 63.

97 Schock, *Unarmed Insurrections*, p. 41.

98 Sharp, *The Anti-Coup*, p. 1.

99 Taylor, Richard K. *Training Manual for Nonviolent Defense Against the Coup d'État*, (Washington, DC: Nonviolence International, 2011), p. 1.

100 Chenoweth and Stephan, *Why Civil Resistance Works*.

101 Bartkowski, Maciej. "Poland: Forging the Polish Nation Nonviolently, 1860s–1900s." in Maciej Bartkowski (ed.). *Recovering Nonviolent History: Civil Resistance in Liberation Struggles*. Boulder: Lynne Rienner, 2011. Print, p. 271.

102 Zunes, Stephen. "How to Discredit Your Democratic Opponents in Egypt." *OpenDemocracy.net*, 17 Feb. 2014.

103 Beyerle, *Curtailing Corruption*, p. 275.

104 Ackerman, Peter, et al. "Ukraine: A nonviolent victory." *OpenDemocracy.net*, 3 Mar. 2014.

105 Chenoweth, Erica. "The Dissident's Toolkit." *Foreign Policy*, 25 Oct. 2013.

106 Sharp, *Waging Nonviolent Struggle*. p. 409.

107 Ackerman and Merriman, *A Checklist for Ending Tyranny*, p. 5.

108 Based on: Sharp, *Dictionary of Power and Struggle*, 2012, p. 114.

109 Zunes, Stephen. "Upsurge in Repression Challenges Nonviolent Resistance in Western Sahara." *OpenDemocracy.net*, 17 Nov. 2010.

110 Kurtz, Lester. "The Mothers of the Disappeared: Challenging the Junta in Argentina (1977-1983)." International Center on Nonviolent Conflict (2010): 1-10, p. 6.

111 Clark, Howard, et al. "Historical uses of nonviolent action." In *Handbook for Nonviolent Campaigns*, Second Edition, edited by Gárate, Javier, et al. London: War Resisters' International, 2014, p. 15.

112 Sharp, *From Dictatorship to Democracy*, p. 22.

113 Popovic, et al. *CANVAS Core Curriculum: A Guide to Effective Nonviolent Struggle*, p. 148.

114 Jul Sørensen, Majken, and Brian Martin. "Freedom Flotilla to Gaza — a dilemma action case study." In *Handbook for Nonviolent Campaigns*, Second Edition, edited by Gárate, Javier, et al. London: War Resisters' International, 2014, p. 171.

115 Based on: Gárate, Javier, et al. *Handbook for Nonviolent Campaigns*, Second Edition, London: War Resisters' International, 2014, p. 226.

116 Center for Campus Organizing, *Organizing Guide of Peace and Justice Groups*. July 1995. http://www.ibiblio.org/netchange/cco/index.html.

117 Sheehan, Joanne, and Eric Bachman. "Seabrook-Wyhl-Marckolsheim: transnational links in a chain of campaigns." In *Handbook for Nonviolent Campaigns*, Second Edition, edited by Gárate, Javier, et al. London: War Resisters' International, 2014, p. 147.

118 Moser-Puangsuwan, Yeshua. "Burma: Civil Resistance in the Anticolonial Struggle, 1910s-1940" in Maciej Bartkowski (ed.). *Recovering Nonviolent History: Civil Resistance in Liberation Struggles*. Boulder: Lynne Rienner, 2011. Print, p. 190.

119 Based on: Sharp, *There are Realistic Alternatives*, p. 32.

120 Lakey, G. (1968). "The Sociological Mechanisms of Nonviolent Action." *Peace Research Review* 2(6): 1–102.

121 Popovic, et al. *CANVAS Core Curriculum: A Guide to Effective Nonviolent Struggle*, p. 62.

122 Bleiker, Roland. *Nonviolent Struggle and the Revolution in East Germany*. Cambridge: Albert Einstein Institution, 1993. Print, p. 32.

123 Schock, *Unarmed Insurrection*, p. 51-52.

124 Stephan, Maria J., ed. *Civilian Jihad: Nonviolent Struggle, Democratization, and Governance in the Middle East*. New York: Palgrave Macmillan, 2009. Print, p. 306.

125 Masullo, Juan. *The Power of Staying Put: Nonviolent Resistance Against Armed Groups in Colombia*. ICNC Press, 2015. Print, p. 8.

126 *Civil Resistance: A First Look*, International Center on Nonviolent Conflict, 2011. Print, p. 7.

127 Based in part on definitions found in *New Oxford Dictionary* and Webster's Dictionary, online.

128 Merriman, Hardy. "The Trifecta of Civil Resistance: Unity, Planning, Discipline." *OpenDemocracy.net*, 19 Nov. 2010. Web.

129 Helvey, *On Strategic Nonviolent Conflict*, p. 16.

130 *New Oxford American Dictionary*.

131 Beyerle, Shaazka. "Digital Resistance for Clean Politicians: Brazil" *Curtailing Corruption: People Power for Accountability and Justice*. Boulder: Lynne Rienner Publishers, 2014. Print, p. 67.

132 Beyerle, Shaazka. "Courage, Creativity, and Capacity in Iran: Mobilizing for Women's Rights and Gender Equality." *Georgetown Journal of International Affairs*, IX, no. 2, 2008, p. 41.

133 Ibid, p. 41-42.

134 Oxford Languages.

135 Sharp, *Dictionary*, p. 123.

136 Watson, Ivan. "China Goes Global in Its Pursuit of Critics." CNN. Cable News Network, 4 Feb. 2016.

137 Kurtz, Lester. "Repression's Paradox in China." *OpenDemocracy.net*, 17 Nov. 2010. Web.

138 Bacic, Roberta. "Chile: Gandhi's insights gave people courage to defy Chile's dictatorship." In *Handbook for Nonviolent Campaigns*, Second Edition, edited by Gárate, Javier, et al. London: War Resisters' International, 2014, p. 150.

139 Schock, *Unarmed Insurrections*, p. 42.

140 Speck, Andreas. "Nonviolence and power." In *Handbook for Nonviolent Campaigns*, Second Edition, edited by Gárate, Javier, et al. London: War Resisters' International, 2014, p. 34-35.

141 Beyerle, *Freedom From Corruption*, p. 14.

142 Zunes, Stephen. "How to Discredit Your Democratic Opponents in Egypt." *OpenDemocracy.net*, 17 Feb. 2014.

143 Based on: *New Oxford American Dictionary*.

144 "The Bangkok Declaration: Restoring Trust," Fourteenth International Anti-Corruption Conference (IACC), November 13, 2010, http://14iacc.org, as cited in Beyerle, *Curtailing Corruption*, p. 26.

145 Schock, *Unarmed Insurrection*, p. 51.

146 King, Mary Elizabeth. "Palestine: Nonviolent Resistance in the Struggle for Statehood, 1920s–2012." *Recovering Nonviolent History: Civil Resistance in Liberation Struggles*. Boulder: Lynne Rienner, 2013. Print, p. 162.

147 Kurtz, Lester. "The Mothers of the Disappeared: Challenging the Junta in Argentina (1977 – 1983)." International Center on Nonviolent Conflict (2010): 1-10. Web, p. 3.

148 Based on: Sharp, *Dictionary*, p. 130.

149 Based on: Sharp, *Dictionary*, p. 130.

150 Popovic, et al. *CANVAS Core Curriculum: A Guide to Effective Nonviolent Struggle*, p. 231.

151 Johansen, Jørgen. "Conflict." In *Handbook for Nonviolent Campaigns,* Second Edition, edited by Gárate, Javier, et al. London: War Resisters' International, 2014, p. 33.

152 Beyerle, *Curtailing Corruption*, p. 273.

153 Bartkowski, Maciej J. "Insights into Nonviolent Liberation Struggles." *Recovering Nonviolent History: Civil Resistance in Liberation Struggles*. Boulder: Lynne Rienner, 2013. Print, p. 344.

154 Stephan, Maria J., "Checklist for External Assistance to Nonviolent Movements" in *Is Authoritarianism Staging a Comeback?*, by Mathew Burrows and Maria J. Stephan (eds.), Washington, DC: The Atlantic Council, 2015. p. 208.

155 Beyerle, *Curtailing Corruption*, p. 280-281.

156 Stephan, Maria J. and Erica Chenoweth. "Why Civil Resistance Works: The Strategic Logic of Nonviolent Conflict." *International Security*, vol. 33, no. 1, 2008, p. 37.

157 Chenoweth, Erica and Maria J. Stephan. *Why Civil Resistance Works: The Strategic Logic of Nonviolent Conflict*. New York: Columbia University Press. 2011. Print, p. 194.

158 Based on: Entman, Robert M. *Projections of Power: Framing News, Public Opinion, and U.S. Foreign Policy*. Chicago: U of Chicago, 2004. Print, p. 5. Entman's definition is: "selecting and highlighting some facets of events or issues and making connections among them so as to promote a particular interpretation, evaluation, and/or solution." We have simplified it here for translators.

159 Ganz, Marshall, "Leading Change: Leadership, Change, and Social Movements" in Nitin Nohria and Rakesh Khurana (eds.), "Handbook of Leadership Theory and Practice: A Harvard Business School Centennial Colloquium" Boston, MA: Harvard Business Review Press, 2010.

160 MacLeod, Jason. "West Papua: Civil Resistance, Framing, and Identity, 1910s–2012." *Recovering Nonviolent History: Civil Resistance in Liberation Struggles*. Boulder: Lynne Rienner, 2013. Print, p. 230.

161 Ibid.

162 Boaz, Cynthia. "Red Lenses on a Rainbow of Revolutions." *OpenDemocracy.net*, 17 Nov. 2010. Web.

163 Ibid.

164 Based on Sharp, *Dictionary*, p. 138 and Oxford Languages: https://languages.oup.com/google-dictionary-en/

165 Sharp, *Self-Liberation*, p. 44.

166 Dorjee, *The Tibetan Nonviolent Struggle*, p. 41.

167 *Handbook on Monitoring Freedom of Peaceful Assembly*. Handbook. Warsaw: OSCE Office for Democratic Institutions and Human Rights, 2011. Print, p. 7.

168 "Freedom of Assembly." *Human Rights House Foundation*. 18 Feb 2019. humanrightshouse.org/we-stand-for/freedom-of-assembly/.

169 Helvey, *On Strategic Nonviolent Conflict*, p. 16.

170 Brett, Roddy. *Guatemala (Ongoing)*. International Center on Nonviolent Conflict, 2008, p. 3.

171 https://www.ohchr.org/EN/Issues/FreedomOpinion/Pages/Standards.aspx

172 Schock, *Unarmed Insurrections*, p. 151.

173 Beyerle, *Curtailing Corruption*, p. 112.

174 Chenoweth, Erica and Maria J. Stephan. *Why Civil Resistance Works*, p. 69

175 Popovic, et al. *CANVAS Core Curriculum: A Guide to Effective Nonviolent Struggle*, p. 16.

176 Clark, Howard, et al. "Historical Uses of Nonviolent Action." In *Handbook for Nonviolent Campaigns*, Second Edition, edited by Gárate, Javier, et al. London: War Resisters' International, 2014, p. 13.

177 Based on: Sharp, Gene. *Self-Liberation: A Guide to Strategic Planning for Action to End a Dictatorship or Other Oppression*, Boston: The Albert Einstein Institution, 2010, p. 47.

178 Sharp, *Self-Liberation*, p. 16.

179 Popovic, et al. *CANVAS Core Curriculum: A Guide to Effective Nonviolent Struggle*, p. 95.

180 Based on: Dictionary.com.

181 Beyerle, *Curtailing Corruption*, p. 187.

182 Dorjee, *The Tibetan Nonviolent Struggle*, p. 53.

183 Based on: Dictionary.com.

184 Kurtz, Lester R. *Chile: Struggle against a military dictator (1985 – 1988)*, International Center on Nonviolent Conflict, 2009, p. 2.

185 Merriman. "The Trifecta of Civil Resistance: Unity, Planning, Discipline." *OpenDemocracy.net*, 19 Nov. 2010.

186 Miller, Christopher E. *Only Young Once: An Introduction to Nonviolent Struggle for Youths*. Addis Ababa: U for Peace, Africa Programme, 2006. Print, p. 43.

187 Sharp, *How Nonviolent Struggle Works*, p. 56.

188 Based on: UN Fact Sheet No. 29 Human Rights Defenders: Protecting the Right to Defend Human Rights.

189 The Declaration's full name is the "Declaration on the Right and Responsibility of Individuals, Groups and Organs of Society to Promote and Protect Universally Recognized Human Rights and Fundamental Freedoms."

190 See the EU Guidelines on Human Rights Defenders.

191 European Parliament. Subcommittee on Human Rights. Policy Department. *Nonviolent Civic Action in of Human Rights and Democracy*. By Véronique Dudouet and Howard Clark. PE407.008. Brussels: European Parliament, 2009. 1-50. Print, p. 16.

192 Declaration on Human Rights Defenders "Declaration on the Right and Responsibility of Individuals, Groups and Organs of Society to Promote and Protect Universally Recognized Human Rights and Fundamental Freedoms." The Office of the United Nations High Commissioner for Human Rights (OHCHR), Apr. 2000. Web.

193 Schock, *Unarmed Insurrections*, p. 161.

194 Svensson, Isak and Mathilda Lindgren. "Peace and Protest: Unarmed Insurrections in East Asia, 1946–2006 by Isak Svensson and Mathilda Lindgren, Uppsala University." *AsiaPortal Infocus*. 30 Oct. 2009. Web.

195 Dudouet, *Nonviolent Resistance and Conflict Transformation in Power Asymmetries*, p. 14.

196 Sharp, *The Anti-Coup*, p. 22.

197 Rigby, Andrew. "Fear." In *Handbook for Nonviolent Campaigns*, Second Edition, edited by Gárate, Javier, et al. London: War Resisters' International, 2014. Print, p. 106.

198 Based on: Sharp, *Dictionary*, p. 167.

199 Based on: Sharp, *Dictionary*, p. 167.

200 Beyerle, *Curtailing Corruption*, p. 184.

201 Helvey, *On Strategic Nonviolent Conflict*, p. 4-5.

202 Stephan, Maria J. "How the Hong Kong Protesters Can Win." *Foreign Policy*, 6 Oct. 2014.

203 Sharp, *Dictionary*, p. 173.

204 Smedjeback, Martin. "Forms of nonviolent action." In *Handbook for Nonviolent Campaigns*, Second Edition, edited by Gárate, Javier, et al. London: War Resisters' International, 2014. Print, p. 124.

205 Beyerle, *Curtailing Corruption*, p. 108.

206 Sharp, *The Anti-Coup*, p. 14.

207 Chenoweth and Stephan, *Why Civil Resistance Works*, p. 36.

208 Sharp, *There Are Realistic Alternatives*, p. 33.

209 Lakey, G. (1968). "The Sociological Mechanisms of Nonviolent Action." *Peace Research Review* 2(6): 1–102.

210 Popovic, et al. *CANVAS Core Curriculum: A Guide to Effective Nonviolent Struggle*, p. 63.

211 Ibid, p. 78.

212 Miller, *Only Young Once*, p. 40.

213 Sharp, *Waging Nonviolent Struggle*, p. 45.

214 Bartkowski, Maciej. "Nonviolent Strategies to Defeat Totalitarians Such as ISIS." *OpenDemocracy.net*, 11 Mar. 2016.

215 Chenoweth, Erica, and Kurt Schock. "Do Contemporaneous Armed Challenges Affect the Outcome of Mass Nonviolent Campaigns?" *Mobilization: An International Quarterly*, vol. 20, no. 4, Dec. 2015, p. 434.

216 Melo, Diego. "2013: The Year of Social Protest and Repression in Colombia (Pt 1)." *Colombia News | Colombia Reports*, 14 Nov. 2013.

217 Hunt-Hendrix, Leah, and Max Berger. "How to Organize After Occupy Wall Street." *The Nation*, 18 June 2014.

218 Based on: Bill Moyer, *Doing Democracy*, Gabriola Island, BC: New Society Publishers, 2001.

Kurt Schock, *Unarmed Insurrections*, Minneapolis, MN: University of Minnesota Press, 2005.

John McCarthy, "Social Movements" in Powers, Vogele, Kruegler, and McCarthy (eds.), *Protest, Power, and Change*, New York: Garland Publishing, 1997.

219 Stoner, Eric. "Participation Is Everything – a Conversation with Erica Chenoweth." *Waging Nonviolence*, 14 July 2012.

220 Merriman, Hardy. "The Trifecta of Civil Resistance: Unity, Planning, Discipline." *OpenDemocracy.net*, 19 Nov. 2010.

221 Miller, *Only Young Once*, p. 45.

222 Conser Jr., Walter H. "The United States: Reconsidering the Struggle for Independence, 1765–1775." *Recovering Nonviolent History: Civil Resistance in Liberation Struggles*. Boulder: Lynne Rienner, 2013. Print, p. 304.

223 Based on: Snodderly, *Peace Terms*, p. 37-38.

224 Ibid.

225 Crist, *Strategic Nonviolent Conflict*, p. 10.

226 Helvey, *On Strategic Nonviolent Conflict*, p. 10.

227 Based on: Snodderly, *Peace Terms*, p. 38.

228 Beyerle, *Curtailing Corruption*, p. 279.

229 Ackerman and Beyerle, *Lessons from Civil Resistance for the Battle against Financial Corruption*, p. 19.

230 Martin, Brian. "Verbal Defence." *Nonviolence Unbound*, Irene Publishing, 2015. p. 146.

231 Pinckney, Jonathan. "Literature Review and Theory." *Making or Breaking Nonviolent Discipline in Civil Resistance Movements*, ICNC Press, 2016, p. 18.

232 Clark, Howard, et al. "Historical Uses of Nonviolent Action." In *Handbook for Nonviolent Campaigns*, Second Edition, edited by Gárate, Javier, et al. London: War Resisters' International, 2014. Print, p. 13-14.

233 "Nonviolence." UNPO: Unrepresented Nations and Peoples Organization, 24 Sept. 2017.

234 Stephan, Maria J. and Erica Chenoweth. "Why Civil Resistance Works: The Strategic Logic of Nonviolent Conflict." *International Security*, vol. 33, no. 1, 2008, p. 10.

235 Irwin, Bob and Gordon Faison. "Why Nonviolence? Introduction to Nonviolence Theory and Strategy." *New Society Publishers*, 1984, p. 5.

236 Mogul, *A Force More Powerful Study Guide*, p. 3.

237 May, Todd. *Nonviolent Resistance: A Philosophical Introduction*. John Wiley and Sons. 2015. p. 45.

238 Based on: Gene Sharp, *Sharp's Dictionary of Power and Struggle*, p. 193.

239 Finnegan, Amy C., and Susan G. Hackley. "Negotiation and Nonviolent Action: Interacting in the World of Conflict." *PON - Program on Negotiation at Harvard Law School*, Harvard Law School, 25 Jan. 2008.

240 Schock, Kurt. "Nonviolent Action and Its Misconceptions: Insights for Social Scientists." *PS: Political Science and Politics*, vol. 36, no. 4, 2003, p. 705.

241 Ibid, p. 708.

242 Based on: Sharp, Gene. *Sharp's Dictionary of Power and Struggle: Language of Civil Resistance in Conflicts*. New York: Oxford UP, 2012. p. 195.

243 Lakey, G. (1968). "The Sociological Mechanisms of Nonviolent Action." *Peace Research Review* 2(6): 1–102.

244 Sharp, Gene. *The Role of Power in Nonviolent Struggle*. Cambridge: Albert Einstein Institution, 1990. Print, p. 17.

245 Schock, *Unarmed Insurrections*, p. 41-42.

246 Dudouet, Véronique. *Nonviolent Resistance and Conflict Transformation in Power Asymmetries*. Handbook. Berlin: Berghof Research Center for Constructive Conflict Management, 2008. Print, p. 15.

247 Helvey, *On Strategic Nonviolent Conflict*, p. 92.

248 Crist, *Strategic Nonviolent Conflict*, p. 11.

249 Based on: Sharp, *Dictionary*, p. 196.

250 Schock, *Civil Resistance Today*.

251 Schock, Kurt. "Nonviolent Action and Its Misconceptions: Insights for Social Scientists." *PS: Political Science and Politics* 36.4 (2003): 705-12. Print, p. 709.

252 Sharp, *From Dictatorship to Democracy*, p. 57.

253 Based on: Sharp, *Dictionary*, p. 197.

254 Schock, *Unarmed Insurrections*, p. 51.

255 Sharp, *Self-Liberation*, p. 62.

256 Sharp, Gene. *How Nonviolent Struggle Works*. Boston: Albert Einstein Institute, 2013. Print, p. 49.

257 Merriman, Hardy. "The Trifecta of Civil Resistance: Unity, Planning, Discipline." OpenDemocracy.net, 19 Nov. 2010.

258 Based on: Sharp, *Dictionary*, p. 204 and Oxford Languages.

259 Chenoweth and Stephan, *Why Civil Resistance Works*, p. 14.

260 Conser Jr., Walter H. "The United States: Reconsidering the Struggle for Independence, 1765–1775." *Recovering Nonviolent History: Civil Resistance in Liberation Struggles*. Boulder: Lynne Rienner, 2013. Print, p. 307.

261 Based on: Sharp, *Dictionary*, p. 204 and Oxford Languages.

262 Jr., Walter H. " The United States: Reconsidering the Struggle for Independence, 1765–1775." *Recovering Nonviolent History: Civil Resistance in Liberation Struggles*. Boulder: Lynne Rienner, 2013. Print, p. 309.

263 Merriman, "The Trifecta of Civil Resistance."

264 Based on: Sharp, *Dictionary*, p. 193.

265 Dorjee, *The Tibetan Nonviolent Struggle*, p. 12.

266 Based on: Sharp, *Dictionary*, p. 208 and *New Oxford American Dictionary*.

267 Ackerman, Peter and Christopher Kruegler. *Strategic Nonviolent Conflict: The Dynamics of People Power in the Twentieth Century*. Westport: Praeger, 1994. Print, p. 43.

268 Stoner, Eric. "Participation Is Everything — a Conversation with Erica Chenoweth." Waging Nonviolence, 14 July 2012.

269 Based on: Sharp, *Dictionary*, p. 208.

270 Helvey, *On Strategic Nonviolent Conflict*, p. 33.

271 Chenoweth and Stephan, *Why Civil Resistance Works*, p. 11.

272 Merriman, Hardy. *Movement Building and Civil Resistance*. University of Denver, Dec. 2016.

273 Principe, *Women in Nonviolent Movements*, p. 7.

274 "Parallel Institutions - Metta Center." *Metta Center*, 28 Aug. 2014. Web.

275 Helvey, *On Strategic Nonviolent Conflict*, p. 85.

276 Crist, *Strategic Nonviolent Conflict*, p. 7.

277 Gárate, Javier, et al. *Handbook for Nonviolent Campaigns*, Second Edition, London: War Resisters' International, 2014, p. 227.

278 Ackerman, Peter and Jack DuVall. "People Power Primed: Civilian Resistance and Democratization." *Harvard International Review* 27.2 (2005): 43.

279 Beyerle, *Curtailing Corruption,* p. 68.

280 Bartkowski, Maciej."Recovering Nonviolent History" in *Recovering Nonviolent History: Civil Resistance in Liberation Struggles*. Boulder: Lynne Rienner, 2013. Print, p. 162.

281 Based on: Sharp, *Dictionary*, p. 219-220.

282 Stoner, Eric. "Participation Is Everything — a Conversation with Erica Chenoweth." *Waging Nonviolence*, 14 July 2012.

283 Helvey, *On Strategic Nonviolent Conflict*, p. 32-33.

284 Merriman, "The Trifecta of Civil Resistance."

285 Duhamel, *The Dilemma Demonstration*, p. 18.

286 Popovic, et al. *CANVAS Core Curriculum: A Guide to Effective Nonviolent Struggle*, p. 87.

287 Ibid, p. 62.

288 Chenoweth and Schock. "Do Contemporaneous Armed Challenges Affect the Outcomes of Mass Nonviolent Campaigns?" *Mobilization: An International Quarterly* 20.4 (2015): 427-51. Web, p. 443.

289 Barreto, José-Manuel. "Mass Political Defiance: A Conversation with Gene Sharp." *Critical Legal Thinking*. Counter Press, 3 June 2011. Web.

290 Sharp likely developed the term "political jiu-jitsu" from Richard Gregg's earlier term "moral jiu-jitsu."

291 Sharp, *How Nonviolent Struggle Works*, p. 120.

292 Sharp, *Self-Liberation*, p. 406.

293 Based on: Sharp, *Dictionary*, p. 226.

294 Sharp, *How Nonviolent Struggle Works*, p. 139.

295 Helvey, *On Strategic Nonviolent Conflict*, p. 38.

296 Based on: *New Oxford American Dictionary*.

297 Based on: *Canvas Core Curriculum*, p. 276 and Sharp, *Dictionary*, p. 229.

298 Sharp, *Self-Liberation*, p. 400.

299 Sharp, Gene. *Social Power and Political Freedom*. Boston: P. Sargent, 1980. Print, p. 24.

300 Based on: "Civic Update: A Matter of Political Space," April 2016, National Democratic Institute, https://www.ndi.org/sites/default/files/Issue%2050%20A%20Matter%20of%20Political%20Space.pdf.

301 Ibid.

302 Schock, Kurt. *Civil Resistance Today*, p. 19

303 Moser-Puangsuwan, Yeshua. "Burma: Civil Resistance in the Anticolonial Struggle, 1910s-1940." in Maciej J. Bartkowski (ed.). *Recovering Nonviolent History: Civil Resistance in Liberation Struggles*. Boulder: Lynne Rienner, 2011. Print, p. 194.

304 Gárate, Javier, et al. *Handbook for Nonviolent Campaigns*, Second Edition, London: War Resisters' International, 2014, p. 227.

305 Merriman, *Agents of Change*, p. 1.

306 Mogul, *A Force More Powerful Study Guide*, p. 4.

307 Beyerle, *Curtailing Corruption*, p. 31.

308 Ibid, p. 102.

309 Ibid, p. 182.

310 Based on: Sharp, *Dictionary*, p. 236 and Oxford Languages.

311 Presbey, Gail. "Ghana: Nonviolent Resistance in the Independence Movement, 1890s–1950s." *Recovering Nonviolent History: Civil Resistance in Liberation Struggles*. Boulder: Lynne Rienner, 2013. Print, p. 53.

312 King, Mary Elizabeth. "Palestine: Nonviolent Resistance in the Struggle for Statehood, 1920s–2012." *Recovering Nonviolent History: Civil Resistance in Liberation Struggles*. Boulder: Lynne Rienner, 2013. Print, p. 162.

313 Based on: Sharp, *Dictionary*, p. 236 and Oxford Languages.

314 Merriman, "The Trifecta of Civil Resistance."

315 Schock, *Unarmed Insurrections*, p. 51.

316 Based on: *New Oxford American Dictionary*.

317 Ishtiaq, Hossain. "Bangladesh: Civil Resistance in the Struggle for Independence, 1948–1971." in Maciej Bartkowski (ed.). *Recovering Nonviolent History: Civil Resistance in Liberation Struggles*. Boulder: Lynne Rienner, 2011. Print, p. 207.

318 Sharp, *Waging Nonviolent Struggle*, p. 176.

319 Pinckney, *Making or Breaking Nonviolent Discipline in Civil Resistance Movements*, p. 20.

320 Ibid, p. 30.

321 Based on: Sharp, *Dictionary*, p. 251-252.

322 Merriman, "The Trifecta of Civil Resistance."

323 Beyerle, Shaazka. *Freedom From Corruption: A Curriculum for People Power Movements, Campaigns, and Civic Initiatives*. Creative Commons, December 2015, p. 14.

324 Schock, *Unarmed Insurrections*, p. 81.

325 Chenoweth, Erica and Kurt Schock (2015). "Do Contemporaneous Armed Challenges Affect the Outcomes of Mass Nonviolent Campaigns?" *Mobilization: An International Quarterly*, vol. 20, no. 4, December 2015, p. 444.

326 Abdalla, Amr and Yasmine Arafa. "Egypt: Nonviolent Resistance in the Rise of a Nation-State, 1805–1922." *Recovering Nonviolent History: Civil Resistance in Liberation Struggles*. Boulder: Lynne Rienner, 2013. Print, p. 136.

327 "A Rainbow of Revolutions." Economist.com, 19 Jan. 2006. Web.

328 Popovic, et al. *CANVAS Core Curriculum: A Guide to Effective Nonviolent Struggle*, p. 82.

329 Kurtz, Lester. *The Anti-Apartheid Struggle in South Africa (1912–1992)*. Conflict Summary. Washington: International Center on Nonviolent Conflict, 2010. Web, p. 1.

330 Stephan, Maria. "Fighting for Statehood: The Role of Civilian-Based Resistance in the East Timorese, Palestinian, and Kosovo Albanian Self-Determination Movements," *The Fletcher Forum of World Affairs*, vol. 30:2, 2006. p. 60.

331 Bartkowski, Maciej J. "Recovering Nonviolent History." *Recovering Nonviolent History: Civil Resistance in Liberation Struggles*. Boulder: Lynne Rienner, 2013. Print, p. 11.

332 Duvall, Jack. "Dream Things True: Nonviolent Movements as Applied Consciousness," *Cosmos and History: The Journal of Natural and Social Philosophy*, vol. 10, 2014. p. 106.

333 Bartkowski, Maciej J. "Poland: Forging the Polish Nation Nonviolently, 1860s–1900s." in Maciej Bartkowski (ed.). *Recovering Nonviolent History: Civil Resistance in Liberation Struggles*. Boulder: Lynne Rienner, 2011. Print, p. 268.

334 Burley, Shane. "Solidarity Networks Spread as a New Alternative to 'Alternative Labor.'" *Waging Nonviolence*, 23 Oct. 2013. Web.

335 Sharp, *How Nonviolent Struggle Works*, p. 108.

336 Moser-Puangsuwan, Yeshua. "Burma: Civil Resistance in the Anticolonial Struggle, 1910s–1940." *Recovering Nonviolent History: Civil Resistance in Liberation Struggles*. Boulder: Lynne Rienner, 2013. Print, p. 185.

337 Sharp, Gene. *Social Power and Political Freedom*. Boston, MA: Porter Sargent, 1980. *Albert Einstein Institution*, p. 46.

338 Ibid.

339 Based on: Brill Olcott, Martha, and Marina Ottoway. "Challenge of Semi-Authoritarianism." Carnegie Endowment for International Peace. Web.

340 Ibid.

341 Ibid.

342 Based on: https://www.lexico.com/en/definition/sit-in

343 Based on: Sharp, *Dictionary*, p. 271.

344 Beyerle, *Curtailing Corruption*, p. 175.

345 Sharp, *Waging Nonviolent Struggle*, p. 202.

346 Sharp, *Waging Nonviolent Struggle*, p. 29.

347 Schock, *Civil Resistance Today*. p. 19

348 Crist, *Strategic Nonviolent Conflict*, p. 8.

349 Kurtz and Turpin, *Encyclopedia of Violence, Peace and Conflict*, p. 573.

350 Sharp, *Waging Nonviolent Struggle*, p. 481.

351 Miller, *Strategic Nonviolent Struggle: A Training Manual*, p. 125.

352 Dorjee, *The Tibetan Nonviolent Struggle*, p. 82.

353 Merriman, "The Trifecta of Civil Resistance."

354 Popovic, et al. *CANVAS Core Curriculum: A Guide to Effective Nonviolent Struggle*, p. 6.

355 Bartkowski, Maciej J. "Insights into Nonviolent Liberation Struggles." *Recovering Nonviolent History: Civil Resistance in Liberation Struggles*. Boulder: Lynne Rienner, 2013. Print, p. 339.

356 Merriman, "The Trifecta of Civil Resistance."

357 Sharp, *Dictionary*, p. 286.

358 Moser-Puangsuwan, Yeshua. "Burma: Civil Resistance in the Anticolonial Struggle, 1910s–1940." *Recovering Nonviolent History: Civil Resistance in Liberation Struggles*. Boulder: Lynne Rienner, 2013. Print, p. 191.

359 Sharp, *How Nonviolent Struggle Works*, p. 65.

360 Abdalla, Amr and Yasmine Arafa. "Egypt: Nonviolent Resistance in the Rise of a Nation-State, 1805–1922." *Recovering Nonviolent History: Civil Resistance in Liberation Struggles*. Boulder: Lynne Rienner, 2013. Print, p. 133.

361 Melo, Diego. "2013: The Year of Social Protest and Repression in Colombia (Pt 1)." *Colombia News | Colombia Reports*, 14 Nov. 2013.

362 Moser-Puangsuwan, Yeshua. "Burma: Civil Resistance in the Anticolonial Struggle, 1910s-1940." in Maciej J. Bartkowski (ed.). *Recovering Nonviolent History: Civil Resistance in Liberation Struggles*. Boulder: Lynne Rienner, 2011. Print, p. 188.

363 Sharp, *How Nonviolent Struggle Works*, p. 35.

364 Pinckney, *Making or Breaking Nonviolent Discipline in Civil Resistance Movements*, p. 53.

365 Schock, *Civil Resistance Today*.

366 Ackerman, Peter and Hardy Merriman. "A Checklist for Ending Tyranny." *Is Authoritarianism Staging a Comeback?* Mathew Burrows and Maria J. Stephan (eds.). Washington DC: Atlantic Council, 2015. 63-80. Print.

367 Bartkowski, Maciej and Hardy Merriman. "Civil Resistance." *Oxford Bibliographies*. 2016.

368 Stoner, Eric. "Participation Is Everything - a Conversation with Erica Chenoweth." *Waging Nonviolence*, 14 July 2012.

369 Abdalla, Amr and Yasmine Arafa. "Egypt: Nonviolent Resistance in the Rise of a Nation-State, 1805–1922." *Recovering Nonviolent History: Civil Resistance in Liberation Struggles*. Boulder: Lynne Rienner, 2013. Print, p. 129.

370 Popovic, et al. *CANVAS Core Curriculum: A Guide to Effective Nonviolent Struggle*, p. 90.

371 Sharp, *Dictionary*, p. 294.

372 Beyerle, *Civil Resistance and the Corruption-Violence Nexus*, p. 73.

373 Principe, *Women in Nonviolent Movements*, p. 3.

374 Beyerle, *Curtailing Corruption*, p. 268.

375 Popovic, et al. *CANVAS Core Curriculum: A Guide to Effective Nonviolent Struggle*, p. 90.

376 Johansen, Jørgen, and Brian Martin. "Sending the protest message." In *Handbook for Nonviolent Campaigns*, Second Edition, edited by Gárate, Javier, et al. London: War Resisters' International, 2014, p. 86.

377 Dudouet, Véronique. *Nonviolent Resistance and Conflict Transformation in Power Asymmetries*. Berlin: Berghof Research Center for Constructive Conflict Management, 2008. Print, p. 15.

378 Taylor, Richard K., "Training Manual for Nonviolent Defense Against the Coup d'État," *Nonviolence International*. 2011.

379 "Nonviolence Training During the U.S. Civil Rights Movement." *Empowering Nonviolence*.

380 Beyerle, *Curtailing Corruption*, p. 174.

381 Lakey, George. "8 Skills of a Well-Trained Activist." *Waging Nonviolence*. 11 June 2013. Web.

382 Miller, *Only Young Once*, p. 62.

383 Based on: Pinckney, Jonathan. *When Civil Resistance Succeeds: Building Democracy After Popular Nonviolent Uprisings*. ICNC Press. 2018. Print and online. p. 15.

384 Karatnycky, Adrian and Peter Ackerman. *How Freedom is Won: From Civic Resistance to Durable Democracy*. Freedom House. 2005. Print and online. p. 4.

385 Pinckney, *When Civil Resistance Succeeds*, p. 10.

386 Pinckney, *When Civil Resistance Succeeds*, p. 24.

387 Beyerle, Shaazka. "Digital Resistance for Clean Politicians: Brazil" *Curtailing Corruption: People Power for Accountability and Justice*. Boulder: Lynne Rienner Publishers, 2014. Print, p. 77.

388 Conser Jr., Walter H. "The United States: Reconsidering the Struggle for Independence, 1765–1775." *Recovering Nonviolent History: Civil Resistance in Liberation Struggles*. Boulder: Lynne Rienner, 2013. Print, p. 307.

389 Sharp, *Waging Nonviolent Struggle*, p. 425.

390 Merriman, "The Trifecta of Civil Resistance."

391 Based on: Sharp, *Dictionary*, p. 306.

392 Sharp, *Waging Nonviolent Struggle*, p. 504.

393 Snodderly, *Peace Terms*, p. 30.

394 Based on: Sharp, Gene. *Sharp's Dictionary of Power and Struggle: Language of Civil Resistance in Conflicts*. New York: Oxford UP, 2012. p. 307.

395 World Health Organization, World report on violence and health, 2002. p. 4.

396 Sharp, Gene. *Sharp's Dictionary of Power and Struggle: Language of Civil Resistance in Conflicts*. New York: Oxford UP, 2012. p. 307.

397 Stoner, Eric. "Participation Is Everything — a Conversation with Erica Chenoweth." *Waging Nonviolence*, 14 July 2012.

398 Ackerman, Peter, and Christopher Kruegler. "The Principles of Strategic Nonviolent Conflict." *Strategic Nonviolent Conflict: The Dynamics of People Power in the Twentieth Century*. Westport, CT: Praeger, 1994. p. 21-53. Print.

399 Chenoweth, Erica and Kurt Schock (2015). "Do Contemporaneous Armed Challenges Affect the Outcomes of Mass Nonviolent Campaigns?" *Mobilization: An International Quarterly*, vol. 20, no. 4, December 2015, p. 427-451.

400 Haines, Herbert H. "Radical Flank Effects." *The Wiley-Blackwell Encyclopedia of Social and Political Movements* (2013). Web.

401 Havel, Vaclav. "The Power of the Powerless." *International Journal of Politics*, 1979.

402 Stoner, Eric. "Participation Is Everything — a Conversation with Erica Chenoweth." *Waging Nonviolence*. 14 July 2012. Web.

403 Chenoweth, Erica and Kurt Schock (2015). "Do Contemporaneous Armed Challenges Affect the Outcomes of Mass Nonviolent Campaigns?" *Mobilization: An International Quarterly*, vol. 20, no. 4, December 2015, p. 437.

404 Beyerle, *Curtailing Corruption*, p. 140.

405 "Platform — The Movement for Black Lives." *The Movement for Black Lives*. Web. 23 Aug. 2016.

406 Based on: Sharp, *Dictionary*, p. 309.

407 Ishtiaq, Hossain. "Bangladesh: Civil Resistance in the Struggle for Independence, 1948–1971." in Maciej Bartkowski (ed.). *Recovering Nonviolent History: Civil Resistance in Liberation Struggles*. Boulder: Lynne Rienner, 2011. Print, p. 204.

408 Based on: Sharp, *Dictionary*, p. 309.

409 Ishtiaq, Hossain. "Bangladesh: Civil Resistance in the Struggle for Independence, 1948–1971." in Maciej Bartkowski (ed.). *Recovering Nonviolent History: Civil Resistance in Liberation Struggles*. Boulder: Lynne Rienner, 2011. Print, p. 204.

410 "Baltimore Student Activists Plan Walkout to Protest Standardized Testing." *Baltimore Sun*. Baltimore Sun Media Group, 14 Apr. 2016. Web.Accommodate (as a result of civil resistance)

Index

A

Accommodate, 17
Accommodation (as a result of civil resistance), 17
Accountability, 18
Activist, 19
Adversary, (see "Opponent") 106
Agency (human agency), 20
Agent provocateur (in the context of civil resistance), 21
Ally (verb), 22
Ally (noun), 22
Alternative institution, 23
Authoritarian rule, 24
Authority, 25

B

Backfire (verb), 26
Backfire (noun), 27
Backlash, 28
Backsliding, democratic (noun), 29
Blockade (associated with civil resistance) (verb), 30
Blockade (associated with civil resistance) (noun), 31
Boycott (verb), 32
Boycott (noun), 32

C

Campaign (verb), 33
Campaign (noun), 34
Capacity (in the context of civil resistance), 35
Civil disobedience, 36
Civil resistance, 36
Civil society, 38
Civilian-based defense, 39
Coalition, 40
Commission, act of or tactic of, 41
Concentration, tactic of, 41
Conditions (see "structural conditions"), 140
Conflict (noun), 42
Consent (political) (verb), 43
Consent (political) (noun), 44
Constructive programme (or "constructive program"), 45
Conversion (as a result of civil resistance), 46
Coup d'état (or "coup"), 47
Crack down (verb), 48
Crackdown (noun), 48

D

Defect (associated with civil resistance) (verb), 49
Defection, 50
Democratic backsliding (noun) (see "backsliding, democratic"), 29
Demonstration (associated with civil resistance), 51
Dictatorship, 52
Dilemma action, 53
Direct action, 54
Disintegration (as a result of civil resistance), 55
Dispersion, tactic of, 56
Disrupt, 56
Disruption, 57
Dissent (noun), 58
Dissident, 59
Dynamics (of civil resistance), 59

E

Empower, 60
Empowerment, 61
Escalate (in a conflict), 61
Escalation (in a conflict), 62
External actor, 63
External support, 64

F

Failure (associated with civil resistance), 65
Flank, violent (see "violent flank"), 153
Frame (in communication) (verb), 66
Frame (in communication) (noun), 68
Freedom (political), 69
Freedom of assembly, 70
Freedom of association, 71
Freedom of speech (or "freedom of expression"), 72

G

Goal, 73
Grand strategy, 73
Grassroots (adjective), 75
Grassroots (plural noun), 75
Grievance, 76

H

Human rights defender (or "HRD"), 77

I

Insurrection, unarmed, 78

L

Leadership, 78
Legitimacy, 79
Loyalty shift, 80

M

March (noun), 81
Mass demonstration, 82
Mechanisms of change, 83
Methods of nonviolent action, 83
Mobilization, 85
Mobilize, 86
Movement, 86

N

Noncooperation, 88
Nongovernmental organization (or "NGO"), 88
Non-state actor (or "nonstate actor"), 89
Nonviolence, 90
Nonviolence, pragmatic, 93
Nonviolence, principled, 94
Nonviolent (or "non-violent"), 95
Nonviolent action, 97
Nonviolent coercion, 99
Nonviolent conflict, 100
Nonviolent direct action, (see "direct action"), 54
Nonviolent discipline, 101
Nonviolent intervention, 102
Nonviolent struggle, 103

O

Obedience, 104
Obey, 105
Objective (noun), 105
Omission, act of or tactic of, 105
Opponent, 106
Opposition group, 107
Organizer (in the context of civil resistance), 107

P

Parallel institution, 108
People power, 109
Pillars of support, 110
Plan (verb), 111
Plan (noun), 112
Political defiance, 113
Political jiu-jitsu, 114
Political noncooperation, 114
Political power, 115
Political space, 116
Political transition (see "transition, political"), 148
Power (noun), 116
Powerholder (or "power holder" or "power-holder"), 117
Pragmatic nonviolence (see "nonviolence, pragmatic"), 93
Principled nonviolence (see "nonviolence, principled"), 94
Protest (verb), 119
Protest (noun), 120

R

Rally (noun), 121
Repress (in the context of civil resistance), 122
Repression (in the context of civil resistance), 122
Resilience, 123
Revolution (social, political, or economic), 124

S

Sanctions (plural noun), 125
Self-determination, 126
Self-organize (verb), 127
Self-organization, 128
Self-reliance, 129
Self-rule, 130
Semi-authoritarian, 130
Sit-in (noun), 131
Skills (in the context of civil resistance), 132
Sources of power, 133
Strategic nonviolent struggle, 134
Strategic plan, 135
Strategize, 136
Strategy, 136
Strike (associated with civil resistance) (verb), 138
Strike (associated with civil resistance) (noun), 139
Structural conditions, 140
Success (associated with civil resistance), 141

T

Tactic, 142
Tactical innovation, 143
Tactical sequencing (or "sequencing of tactics") (noun), 144
Tactic of concentration (see "concentration, tactic of"), 41
Tactic of dispersion (see "dispersion, tactic of"), 56
Third party (or "third-party") (noun), 145
Train (verb), 146
Training (noun), 147
Transition, political, 148

U

Unarmed insurrection (see "insurrection, unarmed"), 78
Unite, 149
Unity, 150
Uprising, 151

V

Violence, 152
Violent flank, 153
Vision (of a civil resistance movement), 154

W

Walk out (verb), 155
Walk-out (or "walkout") (noun), 155

About the Authors

Hardy Merriman is President and CEO of the International Center on Nonviolent Conflict (ICNC). He has worked in the field of civil resistance for over 18 years, presenting at workshops for activists and organizers around the world; speaking widely about civil resistance movements with scholars, journalists, and members of international organizations; and developing resources for practitioners. His writings have been translated into numerous languages.

From 2016-2018 he was also an adjunct lecturer at the Fletcher School of Law and Diplomacy (Tufts University).

Recently, he co-authored the report *Preventing Mass Atrocities: From a Responsibility to Protect (RtoP) to a Right to Assist (RtoA) Campaigns of Civil Resistance*. He has also contributed to several books and co-authored two literature reviews on civil resistance. He further co-authored *A Guide to Effective Nonviolent Struggle*, a training curriculum for activists.

Nicola Barrach-Yousefi has over 15 years of experience working in human rights and with civil society worldwide. She specializes in collaborating with movements and human rights defenders to design field programs and research around human rights, civil resistance, advocacy and hate speech.

She is the Founder and Executive Director of Human Rights Connected, a networked organization focused on mainstreaming understanding of strategic nonviolent action and international human rights law. She also serves as Senior Advisor for Civic Initiatives at the International Center on Nonviolent Conflict (ICNC) and as Senior Advisor for the Hate Speech program at the PeaceTech Lab, including project lead and lead author for the Cameroon, DRC, Ethiopia, and CAR lexicons.

She serves as a consultant for the UN, USIP, and other international organizations.

Published by ICNC Press

International Center on Nonviolent Conflict
600 New Hampshire Ave NW, Suite 710
Washington, DC 20037 USA

www.nonviolent-conflict.org

www.ingramcontent.com/pod-product-compliance
Lightning Source LLC
Chambersburg PA
CBHW072012110526
44592CB00012B/1276